Feminisms in education

Feminisms in education

An introduction

GABY WEINER

Open University Press
Buckingham · Philadelphia

Open University Press
Celtic Court
22 Ballmoor
Buckingham
MK18 1XW

and
1900 Frost Road, Suite 101
Bristol, PA 19007, USA

First Published 1994
Reprinted 1995

A catalogue record of this book is available from the British Library

ISBN 0–335–19052–9 (pb)   0–335–19053–7 (hb)

Library of Congress Cataloguing-in-Publication Data
Weiner, Gaby.
  Feminisms in education : an introduction / Gaby Weiner.
    p. cm.
  Includes bibliographical references and index.
  ISBN 0–335–19052–9   ISBN 0–335–19053–7
    1. Feminism and education. 2. Women—Education—Curricula.
3. Critical pedagogy. I. Title.
LC197.W45 1994
370.19'345—dc20   93–41707
                                                            CIP

Typeset by Graphicraft Typesetters Limited, Hong Kong
Printed in Great Britain by St Edmundsbury Press Limited,
Bury St Edmunds, Suffolk

Women and people of low birth are very hard to deal with. If you are friendly with them, they get out of hand, and if you keep your distance, they resent it.

(Confucius 551–479 BC)

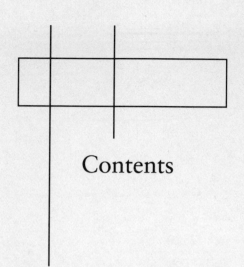

Contents

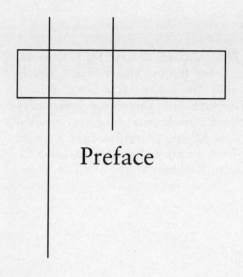

Preface

The chapters of this book cover a range of issues concerning feminism and education. All the material is new although some has appeared in the form of conference papers and those familiar with my work will detect some enduring themes, in particular relating to the work of feminist practitioners. The book therefore can be read as a whole (as the arguments developed form a sequence); however chapters can also be read on their own if readers have a specific interest in one theme. The book has been written to address as wide an audience as possible from practitioners wanting to challenge sexist practice from an informed position to postgraduate students and academics interested in feminist issues; however, others I hope will be attracted to some of the ideas of the book. I have consciously attempted to write in an accessible style often struggling to make complex ideas comprehensible without over-simplification or misrepresentation. If I have succeeded, it is because I have benefited from the help and advice of colleagues, in particular, at the National Foundation for Educational Research and at the Open University.

I would also like to offer particular thanks to the following people who have helped shape the ideas in this book: Dena Attar,

Madeleine Arnot, Stephen Ball, Michael Bassey, Jill Blackmore, Richard Bowe, Agnes Bryan, Leone Burton, Hilary Claire, Wendy Couchman, Miriam David, Judy Dean, Rosemary Deem, Felicity Edholm, Debbie Epstein, Maureen Farish, David Hamilton, Lesley Holly, Alison Jones, Lesley Kant, Pam Lomax, Meg Maguire, Val Millman, Joanna McPake, Kate Myers, Carrie Paechter, Barbara Quartey, Tom Popkewitz, Janet Powney, Iram Siraj-Blatchford, Sandra Taylor, Lucy Townsend, Kathleen Weiler and Lyn Yates.

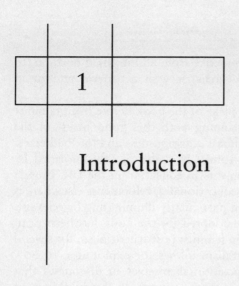

Introduction

As we progress through the final decade of the twentieth century, these are stressful, worrying yet potentially exciting times for those working in education. What ethical and professional challenges face us at this time? How are these different from earlier times? How do we keep equality issues on the educational agenda during an era which, for most of us, appears increasingly state-controlled, antiprofessional and market-led? How can yet another publication on gender help in this?

It is my view, however, that despite the New Right rhetoric of the 1980s and the subsequent 'shell-shock' of practitioners into the 1990s (Weiner 1993), possibilities for pedagogical advance in the context of feminist practice still remain. It is thus a task of this book, by scrutinizing past and present educational discourses, to reconstitute an ethical practice to meet future political and professional challenges and uncertainties.

The main aim of this book, however, is to provide an overview – from a particular feminist perspective – of issues relating to gender, curriculum, pedagogy and practice: for a wide range of people involved in education from those entering the teaching profession, to those reflecting on their practice mid-career or wanting to challenge sexist practice from an informed position, to those studying for higher degrees or with a general interest in feminist issues.

The principal themes and ideas of the book derive from feminist thinking and practice proclaiming both the 'good news' of the transformative powers of feminist consciousness and the 'bad news' of social inequality (Lewis 1990). It is also largely informed by political and policy developments in education in the UK, though drawing on theoretical and educational developments elsewhere if known to me or if they seem particularly illuminating or relevant.

The analytical perspective adopted for the book has been principally shaped by ideas within feminist poststructuralism for several reasons. Feminist poststructuralism allows for exploration of how girls and women actively position themselves in discourses that subordinate them as well as consideration of the workings of patriarchal structures such as the school and education more generally. It also provides an analytical framework for unpacking the micro-political – that is how power is exercised at local (as well as national or international) levels, how oppression works, is experienced and where resistances might be possible (see Chapters 4 and 6 for a more detailed discussion of this perspective).

Gramsci's focus on the importance of *organic intellectuals* serves as a useful starting point here. He argued that the intellectual contributions of progressive groups (such as feminist or socialist educators) are vital for societal change.

> A human mass does not 'distinguish' itself, does not become independent in its own right without, in the widest sense, organising itself; and there is no organisation without intellectuals, that is, without organisers and leaders.
>
> (Gramsci 1971: 334)

It seems to me that if reducing social inequality continues to be a major goal for teachers and other educators, feminist practitioners, as organic intellectuals, will need to continue to analyse and understand policy decisions and outcomes as well as developing their own practice if they are to maintain their challenge to sexist practice.

Feminists working in education have certainly moved forward in the last two decades from the position of having to provide evidence of female disadvantage and gender discrimination in order to enable girls' and women's issues to be placed on the educational agenda to articulating a value-system and practice of feminist education that allows for greater sexual equality at the same time as acknowledging the differences that separate women. In the past, the British perspective on gender has tended to value 'action' over 'explanation' and 'equality' over 'difference' and this was probably an appropriate choice for earlier decades. However, drawing on the work of feminists in the United States, France and Australia in particular, a greater focus on 'difference' and 'explanation' now seems timely, in order to help us clarify the 'problem of girls and women' and how we may move forward into the 1990s and beyond.

In looking at the twin focus of 'equality' and 'difference', I consider two of the most interesting areas of feminist enquiry in recent years: the importance of creating a feminist pedagogy, and how this meshes with theoretical developments within feminism and within educational research to formulate and produce a practice grounded in feminist values or feminist praxis.

A key focus of the book is that of *curriculum* since changes in British education over the last decade have resulted in curriculum emerging as, what Smith (1990) calls, a 'border case': that is, a site of intensive debate which is of crucial interest because it highlights and problematizes taken-for-granted assumptions about knowledge, gender and culture. So, specific curriculum policy orientations need to be considered as emerging at a specific time in history; for example, curriculum policy in Britain in the late 1980s was perceived by Hall (1988) as both 'modernist' and 'regressive'. 'Modernism', he argued, is evident in the attempts to replace 'outdated' social welfare policies of the post-World War II period with free market policies perceived as more in line with the needs of the modern state – and 'regressivism', in the harking back to a former 'golden' Victorian age.

> I'm talking about the taken-for-granted, popular base of welfare social democracy ... Thatcherism was a project to engage, to contest that project, and wherever possible, to dismantle it and to put something new in place.
>
> It is a project ... which is simultaneously, regressive and progressive. Regressive because in certain crucial respects, it takes us backwards. You couldn't be going anywhere else but backwards to hold up before the British people, at the end of the twentieth century, the idea that the best the future

holds is for them to become, for the second time, 'Eminent Victorians'. It's deeply regressive, ancient and archaic . . . It's also a project of 'modernisation'. It's a form of *regressive modernism*.

(Hall 1988: 164)

Regressive modernism is also visible in British curriculum documents of the 1990s where, despite a rhetoric of equal opportunities, there is a failure to address the gendered nature of students' schooling and educational experience. The consequence of this is that when they appear, girls and women (as well as students from black and minority ethnic groups and/or from inner-city areas) continue to be perceived as somehow 'not good enough'.

Curriculum also marks the point where ideas and practice come together within educational institutions. However perceived (see Chapter 3 for a full discussion of this), it is socially constructed and as such, is both a reflection of dominant ideas and a place where these ideas are played out or resisted through practice. One of the arguments of this book is that sexual relations and divisions are likewise formed through ideology and concretized in practice and thus curriculum needs to be viewed as implicated in the definition and construction of gender relations – for example, in defining gender-appropriate behaviour and/or in shaping perceptions of the appropriate place for girls and women in the family, school and employment.

It is, therefore, not surprising that the specific discourses on femininity and masculinity that emerge at different historical periods are visible in contemporary curriculum formulations. Thus in Britain, the 1923 *Report of the Consultative Committee on the Differentiation of the Curriculum for Boys and Girls* (Board of Education 1923), the 1967 Plowden Report on Primary Education (Central Advisory Council for Education in England 1967), *The Education Reform Act 1988* (DES 1989a) which included the establishment of a national curriculum and a 1992 official report on the value of single-sex secondary education for girls (HMI 1992), can all be explored alongside prevailing discourses on, or ideologies about, masculinity, femininity and what counts as 'normal'. In reading them, we can gain insights into how masculinity and femininity have been constructed or produced within and through education in the past, and thus how such constructions may be understood and challenged today.

Thus, a thorough reappraisal of the relationship between gender, curriculum, pedagogy and practice seems timely for a number of reasons:

- The evident need to recreate a feminist practice in education for the 1990s and beyond.
- The impact of the uncertainties of politics and policy in the world context and the ensuing emergence of a variety of new theoretical and political positions including new strands within feminism. In fact, as the title of the book suggests, it is more appropriate to talk of feminisms rather than imply one, unified feminism.
- The importance of acknowledging the considerable achievements of feminist teachers and local government authorities committed to increasing educational equality in the early and mid-1980s which are in danger of being written off in the market-led, corporate climate of the 1990s.
- The relatively recent creation of a national curriculum in England and Wales which has resulted in the re-emergence of 'curriculum' as a pivotal area of policy-making and, consequently, as an arena of debate and conflict.
- The emergence of concerns about the cultural perspectives offered through curricula. For example, in my own work on national curriculum documentation in the UK, I suggest that the curriculum perspective offered remains mono-cultural, male-centred and technocratic (e.g. Burton and Weiner 1990; Weiner 1991b).
- The development of a technology of text production for curriculum policy, used in a particularly powerful and unique way – to create 'teacher-proof' curricula: this is at a time when school teachers are being subjected to what Stephen Ball has termed a 'discourse of derision' (Ball 1990a).

These factors have, together, made necessary the reconceptualization of what counts as feminist practice in education. If the impact of feminist and other equality discourses within education are to continue into the late 1990s and beyond, we need to unpack both the complex set of meanings arising from this variety of factors and their implications for equality issues.

The task of this volume, then, is to restate the aims and achievements of past feminist activists at the same time as exploring the complex arguments emerging from feminist and curriculum theory, for example, those of black feminism, poststructuralism and postmodernism. How can these theories illuminate the situation of the practitioner or the student teacher? How do they differ from earlier conceptions of equality and progress? Or have, indeed, as some claim, all the battles been won? I shall argue that equality issues are still vitally important to the work of education – for students, practitioners and other educationists; that concepts of equality and feminist practice are constantly shifting and mutating; and, with the ever-present possibility of 'backlash' (Faludi 1991), that previous gains need to be sustained at the same time as new campaigns are activated. I shall also argue that poststructural feminist ideas are particularly helpful in enabling us to understand the complexities of curriculum practices.

Furthermore, in arguing that gender relations or the relations between the sexes are discursively constructed, I maintain that the relationships between men and women, girls and boys involve power and domination, powerlessness, submission and resistance. If it is true that biology creates sex differences between men and women, it is also true that notions of womanhood and manhood, femininity and masculinity have a material and social basis. This volume concentrates on how femininity has been produced historically and culturally but it is also important to acknowledge recent, significant work on how masculinity is similarly discursively constructed (e.g. Connell 1989; Hearn and Morgan 1990; Mac an Ghaill 1991).

Like others writing during this period, I also have concerns about the authorial voice and about why the reader should accept my account and analyses of events. What legitimacy does this account have? How can I avoid distortion and inaccuracy, yet maintain a 'balance' between my personal convictions and the field of work that constitutes 'gender and education'? In his work on 'orientalism', similar to feminism in its obliqueness to mainstream scholarship, Said identifies methodological and perspectival difficulties:

> difficulties that might force one, in the first instance, into writing a coarse polemic on so unacceptably general a level of description as not to be worth the effort, or in the second instance, into writing so detailed and atomistic a series of analyses as to lose all track of the general lines of force informing the field, given its special cogency.
>
> (Said 1991: 8–9)

Counter discourses outside feminism such as that of Said can help illuminate the condition of women. As someone who grew up as an 'oriental' in the British colonies, his reflections are helpful in the deconstruction of such terms as 'woman'; for example are 'women', like Said's 'orientals', objects that are historically judged, studied, depicted, disciplined, illustrated, contained and represented? Another link with feminism is Said's criticism of the conception of a 'true' knowledge from which scholars can maintain detachment.

No one has ever devised a method for detaching the scholar from the circumstances of life, from the fact of his [*sic*] involvement (conscious or unconscious) with a class, a set of beliefs, a social position, or from the mere activity of being a member of society.

(Said 1991: 10)

It could be (naïvely!) argued that the male perspectives of writers such as Said are inimical to the feminist project and therefore should be discounted. This is not the stance of this book. Here it is argued that there is no such thing as the 'essential woman' or a 'true feminism'. Instead, it is held that the category of woman is unstable due to its dialectical relationship with other social categories which themselves are continually changing (Riley 1988). As women, we may share certain experiences of sexism and domestic responsibility and we may differ in ethnic origin, class or culture; but what unites most of us is our consciousness that it is other people who set the agenda. Thus what serves to link less powerful social groups are their experiences of 'otherness' and exclusion from the sites of power and meaning-making. This is precisely what Said is claiming is his identification of 'orientalism' as a political vision of reality shaped by the West in which the difference between 'them' and 'us' is promoted.

Hence, though much of this volume is devoted to charting the development of *feminist* discourses within and about British education, other sources will be used where they help illuminate the human, and therefore women's, condition. Additionally, the starting point for the exploration of examining feminist issues in education is that *feminism* has three main dimensions:

- *political* – a movement to improve the conditions and life-chances for girls and women;
- *critical* – a sustained, intellectual critique of dominant (male) forms of knowing and doing;

- *praxis-orientated* – concerned with the development of more ethical forms of professional and personal practice.

The attempt to develop an authorial voice will begin in the next chapter where I select events and influences in an autobiographical journey through the last 20 years as a consumer and producer of educational ideas and curricula. The third chapter examines concepts such as 'curriculum' and 'pedagogy' and the variety of approaches to curriculum analysis, change and evaluation, focusing in particular on two periods in British curriculum history: the large scale national curriculum projects of the 1970s which aimed at persuading teachers to voluntarily change their practice and the more prescriptive government-led curriculum developments of the late 1980s and early 1990s.

Gender issues are foregrounded where possible providing a link to the fourth chapter, where I include both an update of developments in feminist theory and an attempt to read these theoretical developments alongside practitioner and research initiatives relating to gender. The fifth chapter outlines the rich variety of teacher and policy initiatives related to gender over the past decade and a half and how they can be understood in the light of present and future curriculum policy initiatives and analyses. The chapter ends with a relatively brief discussion of how government policy can be understood in terms of feminist values and practice. The sixth moves to the specifics of curriculum analysis and interpretation by exploring the gendered curriculum as a discursive framework in which 'difference' is produced, such that girls and boys, teachers and pupils, different racial and ethnic groups are differently positioned as powerful or powerless, good or bad, feminine or masculine, workers or mothers and so on. It uses poststructuralist frameworks to analyse how gender relations are inscribed within curriculum practices, considering three examples of how such an analysis can be helpful. Two are devoted to specific subject areas (mathematics and science) though in different sectors of education and the third is my own study of British national curriculum documentation. In the latter instance, texts are scrutinized in order to reveal how precise forms of knowledge are produced and presented to teachers; how they are likely to affect current gendered school experiences – of pupils, students and teachers – and how they are utilized for political and rhetorical purposes. The seventh and final chapter explores recent developments in feminist praxis and methodology as a basis for teaching and research, using a particular instance of how feminist praxis was defined and constituted in a research project on staff experience of equal opportunities policies in higher education. All the chapters offer some suggestions for feminist practice and for future action but Chapters 6 and 7 offer specific suggestions for developing an educational politics out of feminist poststructuralism and for creating a feminist praxis as a basis for feminist action.

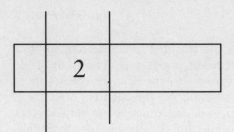

From certainty to uncertainty: an autobiographical narrative

The work that we do and the perspectives that we hold are the products of the interrelationship between personal biography, our place in the social structure, and the cultural milieu and historical period in which we live. Thus our beliefs, values, frames of reference and obsessions should not be viewed only in terms of individual preference or 'individual imagination', as Popkewitz (1988a: 379) suggests, but involve a complex relationship between us as individuals, our communities and the cultures of which we are a part.

Autobiographical accounts such as that which follows can be helpful in furthering understanding about how historical events are played out. By utilizing the narrative structure of biography, they can help us understand changes in historical perspective of, and social conditions in, say, education at the same time as offering frameworks within which personal choices and apparently serendipitous events can be located and positioned. Goodson argues for this approach to be adopted in understanding the work of teachers:

We have to reconnect our studies of schooling with investigations of personal biography and historical background:

above all we are arguing for the reintegration of situational
with biographical and historical analysis.

(Goodson 1981: 69)

However, autobiography-as-knowledge can be highly problematic. Whilst the Oxford English Dictionary views autobiography
as simply 'the writing of one's own history', it is clearly more
complex. Autobiography is necessarily a selection, an ordering, a
shaping; a complex interplay between the present self and the self
recalled at various stages of personal history. Maclure uses the
term *biographical attitude* to describe recent interest in 'person-
oriented genres' for educational research. Biographical attitude,
according to Maclure (1993: 331)

describes a 'slant' or posture towards issues of research, policy
or development which places the biographical subject and
her or his lived experience at the centre of the analytic frame.

However, Maclure warns that autobiographical accounts are
concerned with 'claiming identity' rather than describing experience and that people use them to defend attitudes and conduct, to
make sense of themselves and their actions, to work out where
they stand in relation to others. What is important is that they
cannot be treated as revelations of the honest or unbiased 'self'.
Perhaps, as Grumet (Woods 1993: 462) suggests, autobiography
signifies a wish to ground experience in the personal, as a 'process
of restitution, wresting experience from anonymity and generali-
sation that has dominated the social sciences . . . and returning it
to the particular person who lived it' (Grumet, quoted in Woods
1993: 447–65).

Feminist autobiographical accounts in particular, with their aim
of articulating 'a self-consciousness about women's identity both
as an inherited fact and as a process of historical construction'
(Heilbrun 1989: 18) offer specific and consciously political perspectives on women's lives. So the following autobiographical
account needs to be read as a conscious selection written for a
particular purpose, which can be challenged on the grounds of
interpretation and meaning rather than on the basis of falsification
of a fixed 'truth'.

In this chapter, then, I select some of the events and influences
in my life (personal and professional) set against the main cultural
and political changes in Britain over the past two decades, in order

to provide an indication of how the ideas in this book originated and developed. Since one of the main arguments of this book is that ideas and beliefs are formed and shaped by and within their historical and cultural context, I hope that this autobiographical snapshot will be seen not merely as a self-indulgence or selective recall (or as a process of restitution), but as a means of locating the author's ideas in a specific historical and cultural frame.

I have spent most of my life engaged with education; as a school pupil and college student; as a parent; as a primary schoolteacher and lecturer in higher education; as an educational researcher, writer and editor. Much of my early experience of education – as a pupil and student teacher – occurred at a time of relative prosperity and optimism about the potential of education in promoting social and economic well-being. The Plowden Report (Central Advisory Council for Education in England 1967), signalling a high point in the promotion of 'progressive' teaching methods, was published in 1967, a year before my entry into teacher training, and the relatively high investment in curriculum development during the 1970s enabled me to participate, albeit at a rather late stage, in contemporary curriculum reform debates.

Throughout this time, my views on the purposes, processes and achievements of education were in a state of continual flux and transformation – ranging from an early belief, gained from my mother, in the value and justice of educational opportunity to be grasped at all costs – to a later frustration with, and scepticism about, what I saw as the inherent conservatism of the British education system. As the title to this chapter suggests, the current period is one of uncertainty, where change is swift and immediate and where politics is dictated by the 'photo opportunity' or the proximity of the Conservative Party Conference. It is a period when long-fought gains in the area of education and equality have had to be defended against the harsh conservatism of Thatcherite, market-force government policy – which itself, at the time of writing, is being displaced by a weaker, more conventional conservatism. At the same time, previous epistemological certainties about schooling and the curriculum are being challenged from the political right and the political left: by neo-conservatives as well as by postmodern, critical and feminist theorists.

My cultural roots are important in this context. My origins are middle-European, socialist, and Jewish, and currently my parents' refugee status seems more relevant than in the past. Without doubt, the critical and oppositional stances that I took over the years were profoundly affected by my childhood feeling of 'otherness' or as an 'outsider', for instance, in having parents and relatives who spoke with foreign accents – the north London schools which I attended during the 1950s and early 1960s had not yet developed a conception of cultural diversity or multi-lingualism! Moreover, whilst members of my family were reluctant to talk to me about the reasons why they had been forced to leave their homes at the end of the 1930s, they spent much time arguing loudly and passionately about the necessity of developing a politics of democracy and social justice.

My family were not orthodox Jews and, in fact, most of them were agnostics and atheists. Yet I was encouraged to celebrate my Jewishness – because, as my mother put it, to deny my Jewishness would be to betray all those that died at the hands of 'Hitler' and Nazism including my maternal grandmother, and several uncles and aunts. ('Holocaust' is a comparatively recent term and not in my parents' vocabulary.) All that remains is to note that I was born in May 1944 in Welwyn Garden City, the only child of an Austrian bookkeeper mother and a communist, Yiddish-speaking, sometime actor father of Polish descent. My mother had escaped from Vienna in 1939 to join relatives in London and my father who had been a migrant worker (coal-miner) in Belgium, likewise had fled to England, having been separated from his family at the beginning of the war.

At the time of my birth my father was 'resting' as an actor hence his occupational description of 'dolly-presser' (an ironer of shirt sleeves) on my birth certificate. I was brought up by my mother and her two sisters when my father was deported back to Belgium at the end of World War II – an early victim of Cold War paranoia.

The two main intellectual influences of my life have been what can best be described as the utopian socialism of my family (characterized, perhaps, by the European Socialist parties of France and Italy) and feminism which was 'in the air' throughout my twenties when I became first a mother and then a teacher. Both have survived as influences on my thinking despite my growing distrust of any one political 'truth' or orthodoxy and both have been reflected in my continuing commitment to social justice in education and more widely. If feminism has predominated, it is because at various periods, it has seemed more focused and less ambivalent than other forms of 'progressive' politics. As I have already mentioned, feminism, for me, has three main dimensions – political, critical, and praxis-orientated. These three dimensions of feminism have been variously weighted in the impact they have had on the projects and areas of work with which I have been engaged – as have concerns related to my biography and personal experiences in the educational workplace.

Although, as a child, I was encouraged to think of myself as an achiever, my first remembered 'feminist' feeling was during my first pregnancy at the age of 19. To my horror, I found that as my stomach grew, my personal self diminished so much so that pregnancy seemed to occupy the entire terrain of my existence. For me, like Betty Friedan who called it a 'problem without name' (Friedan 1963), being someone's wife or mother wasn't going to be enough! Whilst only on the fringes of the burgeoning Women's Liberation Movement in London, the reported activities in the press of American activists and Civil Rights campaigners and the appearance of their publications combined with the politically progressive values of my childhood to provide me with a then fresh, particularly 1960s political consciousness concerning equality and change.

The first thing was to get myself an education. In 1968, I gained a place at Sidney Webb College, newly opened to cope with the anticipated teacher shortages of the early 1970s. Although my children were still very young (three years and 18 months respectively) my mother (newly retired from work) offered to share child-care – no doubt recognizing my ambivalence towards the stay-at-home nature of British motherhood in the 1960s. Though my mother died suddenly only a year later, the availability of free nursery places for the children of student teachers meant that I had sufficient child-care support to be able to continue with my studies.

I went to college as a young 'mature' student teacher though I was full of doubts about leaving my children, aware of the unspoken criticism of contemporaries and friends; after all, it was the era of Bowlby's claims about 'maternal deprivation' and the negative effects on infants of working mothers (Bowlby 1953). I was delighted to be training to be a teacher. As the first in my family to experience higher education, unlike Walkerdine (1990), I did not see primary teacher training as a second-rate education or career. Rather, it was my pathway to freedom. I continued to be influenced by feminist ideas, but also began to engage with debates within education, particularly those emerging from sociology and history. I was fascinated by the class analyses of educational sociology, for example that of Olive Banks (1968), though puzzled about why the position of women was viewed so uncritically. My undergraduate honours project concerned an Australian suffragette and socialist, Vida Goldstein, whose unedited papers I had come across in the Fawcett Society Library. Significantly my reading for the project drew me to the liberal feminist ideas of historians such as Josephine Kamm (1965) and Roger Fulford (1958) at the same time as issues of contemporary feminism were highlighted in the work of younger, more radical feminists such as Germaine Greer (1970) and Kate Millett (1971). Thus, though my perspective on Vida Goldstein was celebratory and admiring, I was also able to perceive her as historically positioned, flawed, and her range of activities as reflecting the feminist concerns of the period.[1] Thus, I argued:

> in Vida Goldstein's twenty years of frenzied political activity, it is quite possible to draw a parallel between her life and the contemporary women's movements. When she first began to take an active interest, in the 1890s, the women's movements with which she was most involved, the Australian, American and English Suffrage movements, although not in their infancy, had their most vital work still before them . . . When she returned to Australia and World War I broke out, the suffrage movement died and women all over the world showed in practical terms how much they were worth and their efficiency in doing jobs that men had previously kept for themselves.
>
> (Weiner 1971: 62–3)

I described my subject as a 'woman of conviction' and 'a true democrat', noting her changing political interests – from suffragist and socialist to her conversion to Christian Science. I also saw her as 'politically dedicated . . . a brilliant speaker and organiser' and 'rather sadly, a very attractive lady with very little humour' (Weiner 1971: 40) apparently unaware of the stereotypical trap into which I was falling.

I spent some years as a primary school teacher in inner London trying desperately to apply the 'new' pedagogies of progressivism advocated at college to my classes of 40 plus, simultaneously 'managing' my home and growing family. However, as Walkerdine has pointed out so clearly, the liberation of children conceived in terms of progressivism in education did not mean liberation for the female teacher (Walkerdine 1990). My feminism foundered as I seemed immobilized within the discourse of the primary class-room to challenge the fictions of school-imposed masculinities and femininities. Like Walkerdine's female teachers, I disliked in girls 'the very qualities of helpfulness and careful, neat work which at the same time ... [I] constantly demanded' from my pupils (Walkerdine 1990: 75) finding it much easier to value more de-linquent and destructive behaviour of the boys.

It would not be true to say that I fled the classroom because of these contradictions in my practice. Nevertheless, I was beginning to find the school ethos irksome and oppressive and my submer-gence within it worrying. Thus, whilst still totally committed to my work as a teacher, I sought to try to sort out some of my inconsistencies of practice by embarking in 1975 on a master's course. Again, I focused on feminist issues in my dissertation, this time by researching the background and providing a critique of the then recent sex discrimination legislation. Significantly, I origi-nally chose a different topic as I had assumed that feminist scholarship (or what is now known as 'Women's Studies') was not regarded as a legitimate area of study: it was only at the suggestion of my tutor that I decided to consider girls' education for my dissertation topic.[2]

As is the case for many teachers, my master's year provided me with the opportunity to reflect and take stock, to read and to develop more systematic analyses of the political and social role of education – and to have fun and enjoy being a student again. I remained determinedly cross-disciplinary in my studies, utilizing the ideas of the 'new' sociologists of education such as Bernstein (1971) and Young (1971) as well as the practitioner orientation of Stenhouse (1975). I also continued to draw on the work of a range of liberal and radical feminists (e.g. Firestone 1970; Millett 1971; Mitchell 1971) to formulate a feminist critique of girls' curricula and education generally. At that time, I believed absolutely in the necessity of anti-discriminatory legislation but placed the respon-sibility for changes in classroom practice with the practitioners. I argued that there was an urgent need for both structural and practitioner change in order that courses would be provided 'that will attract women into industries not usually regarded as female territory' and as a result of which 'pupils will be more motivated in school . . . [by] non-sexist teaching' (Weiner 1976: 149, 165).

Following the completion of my master's degree, I headed for the wider, more uncertain world of educational research rather than returning directly to the classroom. It seemed to me that the world of the classroom would be eternally present and that I should grasp any opportunity to widen my experience before returning to teaching. I thus became an educational researcher for the National Foundation of Educational Research (NFER) where I worked on projects concerned with primary record-keeping and vocational courses for non-academic sixth formers. At the NFER, I upgraded my writing and research skills, began to engage with debates within educational research through the British Educational Research Association (BERA) and kept up to date with the few educational initiatives related to gender. These came together in the first ever British conference on gender and education in 1978 held at Loughborough which I helped to organize under the auspices of BERA. Here I was privileged (and awed) to meet, for the first time, researchers and academics who shared similar (feminist) interests to mine. While at the NFER, I had embarked on some preliminary work on girls and mathematics in the primary school and published an article on that subject in one of the two seminal volumes to come out of the conference (Deem 1980; Kelly 1981). My approach at this time prioritized research evidence, dissemination of information and exhortation; thus the article was concerned 'with examining existing research findings on sex differences in mathematics, attributing cause and effect where possible, and then suggesting what consequences these findings have for future action' (Weiner 1980: 56). Surely, I argued, if sexist teachers (whether male or female) understood the harm they were doing, they would consciously try to change their practice.

After several years at the NFER on a series of short-term contracts, I began to feel isolated from the turbulence of teaching. So I returned, not to the school classroom, but to teach on and then to run a government-sponsored Youth Opportunities Scheme in south London. This particular scheme originated from a partnership between voluntary agencies, commerce and industry, and the Department of Employment to provide training and work-placements for local, unqualified school-leavers. It was an illuminating introduction to one of the earlier collaborations between the private and public sectors in the provision of training for the young unemployed. However, the enthusiasm of the participants in the scheme could not hide the complexities of binding education so closely to the demands of the labour market. And the numerous semi-informal business lunches I 'endured' in order to extract placements from business managers served also to remind me whose side I was really on!

Moreover, I was on a short-term (though renewable) contract so was able to move fairly swiftly to the Schools Council to work on the first nationally funded project on gender and education.[3] Despite the election of a Conservative government which was beginning to express hostility to any egalitarian projects, this was an exciting time. The project was a confirmation that gender was beginning to be seen as a legitimate area of educational consideration and it also provided opportunities for influencing the political agenda of education. For this project, information and persuasion still remained the order of the day. The Schools Council Sex Differentiation Project's brief was:

> to seek ways of reducing sex-role differentiation in the curriculum . . . by reviewing and developing existing work on sex differentiation and disseminating examples of 'good' or 'interesting' practice.
>
> (Schools Council 1980)[4]

The assumption behind the project was that teachers discriminated between pupils either because they were ignorant about the implications of their practice or because they were ill-informed about gender issues. Thus remedies were sought to improve the professionalism of teachers by staff development and 'consciousness-raising' – through raising awareness that 'sexism in schools is an educational problem' (Weiner 1985a). Much influenced by Stenhouse's work (1975), the project adopted a teacher-based approach, building on the work of existing 'committed' (namely feminist) teachers in order to identify areas of debate and potential development (reported in Millman and Weiner 1985). While careful to remain within the remit of the Schools Council's objectives for the project, it was also possible to utilize feminist strategies of networking and collaboration in order to offer project support for some of the more radical feminist pressure groups that were developing within education such as the London based 'Women in Education Group' (WedG) and its journal *GEN*. At this time, though removed from the classroom, I identified myself much more with the 'practical' world of the classroom teacher than with the more 'applied' discourses of educational research.

Hence, my work on gender for the Schools Council derived mainly from teacher concerns about gender issues, though also informed by debates within curriculum studies and educational research. Indeed, in the early 1980s, whilst social justice (i.e. 'race') had received some attention within the sociology of education, there was little such discussion elsewhere within education and I was often on my own in raising such issues in seminars and conferences. However, on moving to the Open University in 1982, I became much more aware, through working with feminist sociologists of education such as Madeleine Arnot, Rosemary Deem and Lesley Holly, of the theoretical underpinnings of feminism, particularly those of socialist and marxist feminism. Significantly, I believed that I was contributing a 'practitioner perspective' which I felt was underrepresented in Open University education courses.

One of my concerns at this time was to explore the relationship between feminists' commitment to emancipation and liberation in the classroom and similar concerns expressed by advocates of mainstream teacher-as-researcher approaches. I noted, in a paper published in 1989, some shared interests between the two groups relating to the methods and processes of teacher research – for example, the importance of the relationship between research and the improvement in classroom practice and questions concerning objectivity and validity. However, I also found distinct differences:

> 'Mainstream' researchers (for the purposes of this paper they include Stenhouse, Elliott, Adelman, Kemmis, Nixon, the Classroom Action Research Network etc.) were concerned first and foremost with professional development and improved practice. 'Gender' researchers, on the other hand, were committed to increased social justice within a professional development framework. Further, gender researchers ... related research strategies to ideas drawn from feminist theory.
>
> (Weiner 1989a: 45)

I further observed that the main group of teacher researchers advocated the adoption of practices involving the 'neutral' teacher, the 'reflective practitioner' and 'critical enquiry', yet frequently used the pronoun 'he' to denote the teacher–researcher and also the predominance of males as 'important' authors and theorists. Moreover, the value systems of the two groups were visibly different:

issues, interest in curriculum reform and experience of educational research, and adopting what we called a 'social justice perspective', we developed a policy-orientated and epistemological critique of these texts at the same time as furthering our understanding of the role of text production in curriculum change (Burton and Weiner 1990; Weiner 1991b). In a pessimistic summary of the impact of the new curriculum arrangements, we found little encouragement within the documentation for changes orientated towards greater equality:

> The most practical suggestion we can offer, at this time, is that teachers should continue to try to understand *why* this particular National Curriculum has been imposed at this particular time. In so doing, we may clarify the *purposes* of education and schooling, and the possibilities and limitations for achieving social change through the education system.
>
> (Burton and Weiner 1990: 225)

Additionally, towards the end of 1990, we gained funding from the Equal Opportunities Unit of the European Community to undertake a 'life history' study of black and/or female managers from a variety of educational institutions in order to identify obstacles or enhancements to their career progress.[8] This was my first involvement with the 'women and management' debate though I was already familiar with life history research approaches and their suitability for research topics on women (Mies 1983) and also had been stimulated by the work of some MA students on 'women and power' for whom I was supervisor (later published as Adler *et al.* 1993).

In the event, the 'life history' project provided a fascinating opportunity to extend my understanding of the lives of other education professionals though problems between the black and white members of the research team constituted a sharp reminder of the intersection of the politics of 'race' and gender in social relations. It also revealed the endemic nature of racism as well as sexism in educational institutions and of the need for institutional equality policy initiatives to counter structural inequalities and discrimination. Thus, in reporting on the research, I was able to play a part in the growing debate on the effectiveness of institutional equal opportunities policy-making and implementation (Powney and Weiner 1991).

Funding from the Economic and Social Research Council (ESRC) made possible the development and extension of some of the themes and issues that emerged from the 'life history' study. The resultant project, 'Case Studies in the Development of Equitable Staffing Policies in Further and Higher Education', involved three two-year case-studies of Further and Higher Education institutions with a strong commitment to implementing equal opportunities policies and provided opportunities for engagement with the current management practice (largely male dominated!) and the theories and oppositional writing of feminists (See chapter 6 for a more detailed discussion of this project).[9] It also enabled the research team to enter into appropriate debates relating to the development of feminist or women-friendly research methodologies (e.g. Weiner 1992b). Thus, for example, we explored how feminist research might be constituted and utilized:

> What feminist research can offer to the case-study is a form of *praxis* which engages with social justice/injustice, from the vantage point which might be viewed as more illuminating than other vantage points . . . Further, it calls on the researcher to be reflexive and to ask some . . . questions . . . relating to the scrutiny of data gathering and interpretation.
>
> (Weiner 1992b: 6)

As important, the project enabled *active* participation in institutional policy evaluation, revision and implementation (of equal opportunities) rather than, as in the past, developing a critique from the sidelines!

My intellectual work as outlined in this chapter, then, has been theoretically influenced by debates within feminism and within education. It has also tended to take the form of a *critique*, though the Schools Council project in the early 1980s and the two later management and policy projects were concerned rather more with making change possible and with creating social justice or feminist practice. Also, involvement in a wide range of research and publishing activities over the years – for instance, I was editor of the *British Educational Research Journal* between 1990 and 1993 – generated in me a deep interest in research methodology and the politics of educational research, academic writing and publication.

If I admit to a label, it is that of *material feminism* as explained earlier. I have come to realize that equality issues within education and more widely are more complex than I had first thought and that universal claims are untenable (say, about the experiences of female or black pupils). Nevertheless, I continue to acknowledge the existence of *patriarchal* forces and the resultant patterns of power and subordination, though I now believe that they also cut across and are transformed by class and other social formations. Sadly, I have also come to realize that the 'sisterhood' that was so celebrated in the 1970s is possibly more imaginary than real and that women can be as much divided by class, ethnicity, religion etc. as they are bound together by shared experiences of, say, domesticity and motherhood.

Another challenge to the unitary notion of feminism has been the incorporation, sustenance and development within modern feminism of a wide range of debates (and, frequently, disagreements), for instance, regarding: the role of men and masculinity; the sometimes contradictory perspectives of black and white feminists; changing perceptions of the relative importance of equality and difference; female and male sexuality; variations in feminist perspective, i.e. between marxist, radical, liberal, poststructural feminisms, and so on (Hirsch and Fox Keller 1990).

As the richness of the feminist contribution to scholarship testifies, I *do* believe that feminist theory has been immensely important in asking questions about knowledge, power, nature and wish it were more acknowledged that feminists were way ahead of postmodernists in critiquing the structures and universalities of modernity. Moreover, the relative success of feminism appears to indicate more than just the advancement of women. Thus, as Juliet Mitchell (1986: 36) claims,

> Our situation as women at any given time may not only be a general index of social advance towards a humane and equitable society but a more sensitive (and problematic) indication of the stage of the process of change.

However, I also accept that the *form of feminism* that was espoused by those active in Britain in the 1970s and 1980s is historically and culturally specific and that new generations of feminists will create new forms. New feminisms are inevitable as different social and economic formations emerge. So, whilst the acknowledged project of promoting the interests of women up the power structure is still visible, the feminist meta-narrative/certainties of feminism/tendencies to universality are beginning to be displaced by a plethora of feminisms concerning, for example, the *different voices* and multiple subjectivities of women (Walkerdine 1990); developments in feminist *standpoint* theory (Harding 1986; Hill Collins 1990); interest in the *local* (Probyn 1990); the perception that we are entering a period of *changed ideas*, metaphors and hopes for women (Harraway 1990) and so on.

So, what *is* the future for feminism within education, or outside for that matter? First, it seems to me that it is *uncertain*, though feminism, undoubtedly, will continue in some form and, it is hoped, grow stronger. It is likely, however, to continue to fragment unless an issue emerges that will unite women (such as the Greenham campaigns against cruise missiles in Britain in the 1980s) or unless feminist concerns receive some form of support from the state – though state sponsorship for feminist projects can generate yet another set of problems about ownership of research or scope allowed for critical viewpoints. It seems to me that we must take care not to lose the knowledge we have so far gained, for example, in exploring and developing feminist epistemological forms and in creating new ways of knowing. We must also build on what we have learnt from political campaigns, organizing and networking.

One of the strengths of feminism is that it has legitimated the private as well as the public; thus, this autobiography would be incomplete without some reference to the private sphere. So, alongside the activities described above, perhaps it should be noted that I am now divorced, my children have grown and become (almost) independent and I have entered the mid-period of a woman's life – when she is known as 'of a certain age'!

So, what can be drawn from the above autobiographical selections which will help in understanding the ideas emerging in the following chapters? What can be made of the 'identity' that has been constructed? Perhaps readers may develop an understanding of how certain political perspectives grow and change over time; or appreciate the necessity of understanding the context of the author in order to extract meaning from the text; or, as they dip into the following chapters, take the chance to reflect on how their own perspectives and ideological frameworks have altered and developed over time. On the other hand, they may wish to focus, as Sanders (1989) suggests, on the interesting questions in women's autobiographical writing: on the 'absences' in my autobiographical account; on what has been stressed or left out; on any evasiveness in portraiture; on the existence of a subtext; on what to accept at face value and how much to read between the lines – and, accordingly, then to make their own evaluations and to draw their own conclusions.

Notes

1 Originally entitled 'Vida Goldstein and her work for the international suffrage movement' in 1970, it was later published as 'Vida Goldstein: The woman's candidate' by Dale Spender in her (1983a) edited volume *Feminist Theorists*, London, Women's Press.

2 My tutor was Professor Denis Lawton at the Institute of Education to whom I shall always be grateful for this advice; Weiner, G. (1976) Girls' Education, the Curriculum and the Sex Discrimination Act. Unpublished MA dissertation, London University Institute of Education.

3 The Schools Council for Curriculum and Examinations was established in 1964 'to reappraise syllabuses and curricula'. The Sex Differentiation Project was a small project established during the second phase of the Schools Council after its reorganization in 1978.

4 The two other members of the project team were Val Millman and Kate Myers.

5 The team involved in producing *Girls into Mathematics* included Leone Burton, Pat Drake, Lynne Grahame, Judy Ekins and Margaret Taplin.

6 The thesis, eventually presented at the Open University in 1991, was entitled 'Controversies and Contradictions: Approaches to the Study of Harriet Martineau 1802–76'.

7 The Inner London Education Authority, which as its name suggests, was responsible for education in the central London area and had led the way in developing policies to challenge educational inequalities, was broken up in 1991 (as a consequence of a late addition to the 1988 Education Reform Act).

8 The research team included Agnes Bryan, Leone Burton, Barbara Quartey and Janet Powney.

9 The project team included Maureen Farish, Joanna McPake and Janet Powney.

3

Teacher-proof or teacher-led: universal or specific – discourses on the curriculum

Background

What do we mean by the term 'curriculum'? How is it related to 'pedagogy'? How is the curriculum implicated in the construction of gender relations and inequalities? How can we understand the emergence of current curriculum orthodoxies alongside, for example, nineteenth-century assumptions about school knowledge, early twentieth-century child-centredness or the teacher-focused initiatives of the 1970s? What links are there between ideas about the curriculum, and social and economic events? As mentioned in the introduction, two specific eras of attempts at curricular reform in Britain provide the basis of this chapter: the large scale national Schools Council curriculum projects of the 1970s and the more prescriptive government-led curriculum developments of the 1980s and early 1990s. The contrasting nature of the two approaches to curriculum change adopted in the two eras – the first focusing on teacher autonomy and improvements in professional practice and the second, on improved standards of teaching through greater teacher control and curriculum prescription – serve to highlight and exemplify continuing themes of curriculum and pedagogy and their application to gender issues, as we shall see later in the chapter.

I entered this particular debate, as we have already seen, when I became involved in two Schools Council projects, the first on record-keeping in the primary school (1976–8) based at the National Foundation for Educational Research and the second on gender (1981–2) based at the Schools Council. Both projects were concerned with teacher development, both drew on the centre-periphery model of curriculum development (see later in this chapter) and both vested responsibility for curriculum with the practitioner. The record-keeping project was initiated immediately after Prime Minister James Callaghan's speech at Ruskin in 1976 which signalled, at the end of the long post-war boom, an increasing concern for value for money in education. Record-keeping was construed as a means of revealing (and defending) what teachers actually achieved in the classroom; thus the anticipated guidelines and recommendations from the project were aimed at conciliating demands for greater teacher accountability (Clift *et al.* 1983). And, as we saw in the last chapter, the gender project was concerned with raising awareness amongst teachers and other education professionals about the inequities of sex-role typing and sexism in education (Millman and Weiner 1985).

In the event, in 1981, Margaret Thatcher's 'guru' and her second Secretary of State for Education, Keith Joseph, announced the closure of the Schools Council while I was working on the gender project and I (among others) was obliged to look for other forms of gainful employment. In fact, the closure of the Schools Council marked the end of a particular period of curriculum enquiry in Britain, a 'golden age' (Richards 1978) which had jointly involved central and local government, and educational professionals, and which had marked a high point of professional influence on school reform. Later, this period of professional domination of curriculum development was characterized as having failed, by some, because the curriculum continued to remain 'hidden' – the sole property of the teachers – and by others because it had not sufficiently challenged the status quo and prioritized educational equality as a curriculum and pedagogical issue (Burton and Weiner 1990).

Throughout the middle and late 1980s, after the closure of the Schools Council, the context began to change as an increasingly centrist government took a more directive stance towards education, particularly in its relationship with local education authorities (LEAs) and teachers. Strategies used by the government included that of targeted (or categorical – see Harland 1987) funding, for example, through the Technical and Vocational Educational Initiative (TVEI). Here, government strengthened its power to implement policies on curriculum, assessment and examinations by using the promise of funds to elicit 'a creative response by LEAs and schools' to curriculum review and change (Burchell 1989: 6). The 1988 Education Reform Act (ERA) further centralized the design and control of the curriculum with the inclusion of a framework for a national curriculum. The legislation signalled an end to the decades of teacher autonomy and, according to MacLure (1990: v), expanded authority of central government such that:

> [it] increased the powers of the Secretary of State for Education and Science . . . It restored to the central government powers over the curriculum which had been surrendered between the Wars, and set up formal machinery for exercising and enforcing these powers and responsibilities.

Significantly, teacher organizations and unions were excluded from the nominated membership of working parties established to develop the details of curriculum content (Burton and Weiner 1990).

The legislation, nevertheless, provided a new role for those practitioners, researchers and academics who had retained their interests in curriculum beyond the 'golden age'. They now had a new focus – investigation and analysis of policy implications, contents and workings of the newly emergent national curriculum. How were they to understand the new curriculum era? How did it relate to previous curriculum concerns and curriculum models? Feminists, in particular, were concerned with exploring how prevailing discourses on gender intersected with the curriculum discourses made explicit in the national curriculum documentation.

This chapter, then, is devoted to briefly explicating the historical development of thinking about the curriculum and its relationship to pedagogy, and then considering the proliferation of curriculum models and debates which emerged in Britain during the 'golden age'. It further reviews recent, more managerial, curriculum perspectives tentatively applied in the early and mid-1980s and culminating with the emergence of a prescribed, written curriculum. Throughout, I shall attempt to foreground gender issues though it should be understood that gender issues have been implicit rather than explicit in mainstream (male-stream?) curriculum concerns. Moreover, I shall emphasize the need to understand the *historical specificity* and *cultural embeddedness* of the ideas and theories emerging from discussions about curriculum, and education more generally.

Meanings and definitions

How are various approaches to curriculum and pedagogy to be described and explained? How can they be defined? How do 'curriculum' and 'pedagogy' differ? How are they linked to social changes outside schooling? Hamilton suggests that changes in forms of schooling are closely related to industrial processes. He poses the question:

> Was the changeover from individualized class teaching anything to do with the contemporaneous switch from 'domestic' to 'factory' production ... Similarly was the twentieth-century changeover to forms of individualization anything to do with the introduction of 'scientific management' into industrial production?
>
> (Hamilton 1989: 4)

However for most writers on curriculum, its social origins and practices appear not to be a central issue. Rather they seem to have become embroiled in endless discussions over definitions, particularly about the precise meaning of the term 'curriculum' and about its relationship with 'pedagogy'. The intention here, however, is not to enter these debates but rather seek to understand the meanings attached to various claims on terminology. What do claims that curriculum is synonymous with subject content or syllabuses tell us, say, in comparison to those who claim a far broader meaning? Carr suggests that:

> In the English-speaking world, 'curriculum' is often used in a narrow and traditional way to refer to the content or subject matter that is transmitted to pupils by teachers and schools. Where curriculum is defined in this way – as synonymous with 'syllabus' – curriculum studies is usually little more than a study of the practical problems to which the 'delivery' of the curriculum gives rise and 'curriculum'

debate is a narrow technical debate about the instrumental effectiveness of different pedagogical techniques.

(Carr 1993: 5)

The suggestion here is that how certain terms are defended signify implicit assumptions about educational ideologies and practices. A revealing illustration of this is the way in which all official documentation on the British national curriculum since the 1988 legislation (e.g. Ofsted 1993) conceptualizes curriculum as meaning *only* delivery of the national curriculum.

Pring argues for a broader definition of curriculum, based on professional assumptions about the positioning of teachers in curriculum discourses and the relationship between syllabus and pedagogy:

> By the curriculum I mean simply the learning experiences that are planned within the school. Often there are happenings, events which may not be part of the overall plan. I do not want to include these in the curriculum, even if they may be of educational interest. The notion of a plan, of a scheme, of a programme ... tried out (by the teachers) and subsequently evaluated, improved or abandoned, is central ... to this book.

(Pring 1989: 2)

Within this professional curriculum discourse, *deliberation* and *intentionality* are emphasized. In a similar fashion to Pring, Skilbeck (1989: 4) imbues curriculum with purpose and order as 'the principal means whereby the school pursues its educational purposes and organises and structures learning'.

Discourses on the curriculum, such as those of Pring and Skilbeck, produce the term 'curriculum' as 'real', fixed and neutral. They do not allow that such meanings may be fought over and remade according to prevailing views about how to create 'the good society'. Carr takes a different view:

> The way in which the curriculum is made and remade – the process of curriculum change – is essentially a process of contestation and struggle between individuals and social groups whose different views about the curriculum reflect their differences about the good society and how it may be created.

(Carr 1993: 7)

Feminists, among others, have been more likely to see the curriculum as a site of struggle and contestation, and have therefore been active in developing alternative meanings which point up power relations and inequalities that suffuse curriculum formulations and relations. Moreover, they have tended to focus rather more on the possibilities of pedagogical rather than curriculum change. Kenway and Modra provide a warning about adopting a term that has a variety of meanings derived from a particular set of uncritical educational practices. For them, 'pedagogy' is conventionally:

> a term little used by teachers and much used by academics talking about the components of the act of classroom teaching. Often such discussion rests upon an instrumental, transmission model of teaching which fails to make problematic either the learner, teacher or knowledge, or the relationship between them.
>
> (Kenway and Modra 1992: 140)

Nevertheless, as we shall see in Chapter 7, feminists have sought to transform notions of pedagogy to accommodate feminist understandings about epistemology and classroom practices. For example, drawing on discourses of critical pedagogy 'grounded more self-consciously in histories and theories of education and social thought generally', they have tried to construct a feminist critical pedagogy in order to create 'the emancipatory classrooms we had come to believe were both desirable and possible' (Luke and Gore 1992: 9). Lusted exemplifies this more complex and active perspective on pedagogy, as one where 'the transformation of consciousness . . . takes place at the intersection of three agencies – the teacher, the learner and the knowledge they gather to produce' (quoted in Lather 1991: 15). However, these are comparatively recent ideas about the place of curriculum in the schooling process. What now follows is a brief (and admittedly partial) chronological overview of changes in conceptualization of curriculum and pedagogical issues, to provide a backdrop to more recent contestations and transformations in curriculum practices, discussed later in the chapter.

Viewing the curriculum historically

Before the Enlightenment at the end of the eighteenth century, the western conception of curriculum and schooling was principally as a means of promoting spiritual deliverance in which Bible study formed the basis of all worthwhile knowledge. Later, as the study of 'nature' replaced biblical studies, and 'reason' replaced 'belief', modern, more familiar forms of knowledge began to emerge. Thus teaching and learning became secular as opposed to theological, and contemporary developments in the growth of scientific and social knowledge began to infiltrate post-Enlightenment curriculum thinking. These included notions such as:

- curricula should be represented as a *selection* from available knowledge (as knowledge about the world increased);
- there should be *differentiated* curricula for different social groups (as new class formations emerged);
- the *functionality* (or usefulness) of curricula should be emphasized;
- curricula should be developed with the aim of promoting *social advancement* rather than merely with ensuring continuity of the existing social order.

These four features of curriculum thinking – selection, differentiation, functionality and social advancement – as you will see, are as visible as ever in more recent curriculum formulations.

Moreover, curriculum development was, by definition, a *planned* affair crucially influenced by Cartesian ideas of 'order' and 'method'. Hamilton (1989) locates the earliest source of 'curriculum' in the records of Glasgow University in 1633, connecting its presence to the emergence of Protestantism and Calvinism and to assumptions about the necessity for social efficiency. Furthermore, these influences are clearly visible in contemporary interpretations of curriculum as 'the entire multi-year course followed by a student' (Hamilton 1989: 45). These developments were followed by the rise of feminism in Western Europe in the late eighteenth and nineteenth centuries, this time associated with the emergence of liberal Protestantism and religious individualism, and with the evolution of ideas about natural rights, justice and political democracy (Banks 1981).

Thus by the nineteenth century, the two opposing themes of order and control and rights and freedom began to infuse (and clash within) curriculum thinking. Curriculum began to develop stronger social undertones, leading, as Lawton points out, to the emergence of two distinct nineteenth-century traditions: those of the 'public/grammar' and 'elementary' schools.

On the one hand there was the public school/grammar school tradition of education for leadership, which gave rise to a curriculum for 'Christian gentlemen' who would become the leaders of society – managers in industry at home, or district officers in the colonies . . . On the other hand the elementary school tradition was especially intended for the lower orders. Elementary schools were designed to produce a labour force able to understand simple written instructions and capable of making elementary calculations.

(Lawton 1975: 1)

Interestingly, as Lawton's work exemplifies, statements about curriculum tended to exclude consideration of the specific schooling and educational experiences of girls and young women. They overlooked, for example, the two parallel *female* curriculum traditions of the nineteenth century which related to both gender and class: the first based on Victorian middle-class assumptions concerned 'the perfect lady' and the second, her hard-working, proletarian sister, 'the good woman'. The curriculum for these stereotypical, nineteenth-century educational products was framed according to the skills, knowledge and accomplishments thought necessary for their adult lives; thus household management was reserved for the future 'lady' of the house and laundry skills, for the future working 'woman'. Moreover, the teaching of such skills, knowledge and accomplishments was incorporated in various frameworks of knowledge to be learnt by the female pupil.

The female curriculum was invariably linked to girls' biology and their eventual domestic destinies within the family, exemplified in the claimed link between female 'over-education' and infertility (Delamont and Duffin 1978). In contrast, male-as-norm curricula focused on boys' public roles, in the labour force and as citizens. Moreover, throughout the nineteenth century, where education and schooling were considered an option for girls and women, two perspectives predominated. The first and most popular view was that women were *different* from (and inferior to) men, not only biologically but socially, intellectually and psychologically. Hence, according to this view, girls needed an education different from that of boys, which related specifically to their inferior roles in society. A subbranch of this view was that women were different from, yet complementary and of equal status to, men – a rhetoric that was never translated into practical action though was evident in later curriculum documentation (e.g. Board of Education 1923).

The second view (held by most feminists of the period) was that if girls and women were educated equally with boys and men, they would be able to assume their rightful place in society as the social and intellectual *equals* of men. In practice, however, the Revised Code (1862) placed elementary working-class girls on an equal footing with boys. The amount of money earned by successful examination results was the same for girls as for boys. With the relaxation of the code, new gender-specific subjects were introduced: for girls – in the 1870s, sewing, knitting and cookery (theoretical!) and in the 1880s, laundry work, dressmaking, home nursing, elementary hygiene and physiology, and for boys – more mathematics and technical drawing. In contrast, apart from the few girls who attended the newer girls' grammar schools, most middle-class girls languished in academies learning 'accomplishments' (e.g. piano-playing, etiquette) to prepare them for the social setting of the drawing room and parlour.

By the first decades of the twentieth century, however, growing interest in the operations of the mind and, in particular, in the work of Sigmund Freud, began to transform understandings about the curriculum. Perceptions of the importance of the framework of the *learner* started to displace previous conceptualizations of curriculum based exclusively on realms of knowledge. For example, the new discipline of psychology influenced the emergence of the notion of a child-centred curriculum, and promoted child development in curriculum design, drawing on the work of Montessori and Froebel (reported in Hamilton 1990). From the USA, early twentieth-century 'democratic' educational thinkers such as John Dewey (see Dewey 1966) began to stress the importance of developing a 'child-centred' curriculum according to the unfolding nature of the child, this time, drawing on the work of the romantic, Enlightenment ideas of Rousseau.

Simultaneously, shifts in the school curriculum were being forced by the new work opportunities open to women, such as typewriting, clerical and telephonic work – despite the fact that the main purpose of female education was still thought to be for motherhood and domesticity. Significantly, the Board of Education (1923) *Report of the Consultative Committee on the Differentiation of the Curriculum for Boys and Girls* attempted to reconcile contemporary moves towards sex-equality (notably, extension of the franchise to women in 1918 and 1929) with contemporary ideas from psychology. The different but equal theme was well-defended:

> We can afford to recognise that equality does not demand identity but is compatible with, and even depends upon, a system of differentiation under which either sex seeks to multiply at a rich interest its own peculiar talents. Dissimilars are not necessarily unequals; and it is possible to conceive an equality of the sexes which is all the truer and richer because it is founded on mutual recognition of differences and equal cultivation of different capacities.
>
> (Board of Education 1923)

Whilst the report criticised the schools of both sexes for offering too academic a curriculum, it was girls that were held to need a more practical curriculum because they were physically weaker: 'one of the most important aims of training, that of fitting girls for the duties of motherhood and for work in the home, has been unduly obscured by the academic trend' (Board of Education 1923).

A recurrent theme, noticeable both in nineteenth and twentieth-century discourses on women's education, was an apparently genuine fear that the workings of the female mind were in conflict with the workings of the female body, and that, somehow, *academic* work will inevitably intervene and destroy woman's natural destiny as wife and as mother (Delamont and Duffin 1978).

By the early post-World War II period, the importance of education for an advanced industrial power began to emerge as a new curriculum discourse, such that interest developed in the role of school curricula in aiding the creation of a more highly skilled labour force. Not unexpectedly given the then recent experience of global conflict, official documents stressed the unity of purpose of the school curriculum. As the 1940s progressed, the need was identified for a wider choice of courses to meet the requirements of different levels of student ability, interest and attitude particularly in the secondary school. Further, as single subjects replaced group examinations which had dominated the secondary curriculum to 16, schools were left freer to plan their own curriculum (Gordon 1978). Nevertheless, there were those, such as the members of the Council for Curriculum Reform, who criticized this free-for-all approach, arguing for a more purposeful curriculum which reflected the wishes of 'society'. Gordon (1978: 2) describes their position as follows:

> The curriculum ... should be seen as an instrument devised
> for a purpose. If society wants unity, it will provide for
> common experience in pre-adult life: if it wants a division in
> society it will provide different types of curricula for differ-
> ent schools and if it doesn't know what it wants, its educa-
> tion system will reflect the social chaos.

During the 1940s and 1950s, education was by no means the
political football it subsequently became in the 1980s and 1990s.
In fact, there was little difference expressed between the major
political parties on educational policy between 1945 and 1964 as
the relatively few parliamentary debates on education during this
period testify. Moreover, even during the heights of socialist policy-
making of the Attlee administration, gender relations were never
brought under scrutiny, as Dean (1991) points out, and conventional vocational destinations of men (in the workplace) and women
(in the home) were endorsed, without question.

Thus, during this early post-war period, the most influential
debates about curriculum came from North America: from 'professional' curriculum theorists in the form of Bloom's *Taxonomy
of Educational Objectives* (1956) and Tyler's *Basic Principles of
Curriculum and Instruction* (1949) both of which stressed the
'objectives' approach to curriculum planning. Later, Bruner's
emphasis on structure in curriculum planning in his books *Process
of Education* (1960) and *Towards a Theory of Instruction* (1966)
provided an alternative perspective for teachers and curriculum
developers.

However, these theorists were involved in a curriculum debate
that was, in the main, divorced from classroom practice. In identifying this approach to curriculum planning, Goodlad suggested
in 1967 that it had three prevailing features: first, a strong political orientation (rather than broad professional/idealistic goals) –
particularly in gaining funds for curriculum development; second,
an aim of devising at the instructional level a curriculum that was
'teacher-proof'; and third, an emphasis on the technology of
shaping subject matter for learning and teaching rather than on a
broader focus which included the whole school curriculum (reported in Gordon 1978).

In the following decades, during the boom years of the 1960s
and early 1970s when there was, possibly uniquely in the history
of schooling, a high level of public investment in curriculum change,

curriculum innovators reacted both to the disciplinary approach to curriculum as outlined by Goodlad and to the psychological and psychometric views of intelligence formulated in the earlier decades of the century (Wiseman 1967). This twin reaction was to become visible in the funded curriculum reform projects generated in 'a decade of planned educational change' (MacDonald and Walker 1976: 1) starting in 1964 which will form the basis for the next section of this chapter. Significantly, this decade of curriculum reform had been foreshadowed in 1961 when a private charity, the Nuffield Foundation, gave some money to a group of science teachers to develop an aspect of the science curriculum. According to MacDonald and Walker, the Nuffield initiative 'set the wheels of the state turning' which had as its outcome, the establishment of the Schools Council.

Curriculum development and reform: the work of the Schools Council

The Schools Council was the main curriculum development body in the UK between 1964 and 1982, sponsoring approximately 180 curriculum development projects during its lifetime. In order to appreciate the circumstances in which the Schools Council operated – and also the extent to which they differed from current educational assumptions and practices – it is important to note the principal imperatives driving education at this period. MacDonald and Walker (1976) identify a range of social and educational factors reliant on curriculum reform, including: the raising of the school leaving age to 16; trends towards comprehensive schooling and towards larger secondary schools; a general mood of reform; expansion of the local authority advisory services; changes in the secondary examination system; pedagogical shifts towards team-teaching, integrated studies, mixed ability teaching etc. and a sense of crisis in education with the publication of the Black Papers.

Thus, early projects such as 'Courses for the Young School Leaver', 'Sixth Form Curricula', 'Primary French' and 'Mathematics for the Majority' signalled and exemplified the politically progressive ethos of the curriculum innovators of the period. Later, more theoretically ambitious initiatives such as the 'Humanities Curriculum' and 'Integrated Studies' projects were perceived as inducing a clash of values between the intellectually-aspiring, academically-orientated project team members and more conventional subject practitioners in the schools (Gordon 1978).

Also, during this period, much effort was spent on detailing different models of curriculum development, implementation and evaluation. Exemplified in Havelock's (1971) three models of change – social interaction; research, development and diffusion; problem-solving – and Schon's (1971) three models of diffusion – the centre-periphery model; the proliferation of centres model; the shifting centres model – this signalled a technocratic shift in the discourse of curriculum. Emphasis was placed on creating rational and effective models of curriculum change. Thus, the implicit model of planned change held by the Schools Council was centre-peripheral in that the process of curriculum change, both invention and production, was centrally controlled and managed. Curriculum evaluation became increasingly important as the national purse diminished though, interestingly, the discourse of evaluation simultaneously became more political. For example, Hamilton *et al.* (1977: 25) drew attention to the profoundly political and contested nature of curriculum, and particularly of evaluation:

> Evaluation entails a view of society. People differ about evaluation because they differ about what society is, what it can be and what it ought to be. Much of the debate about evaluation is ideology disguised as technology.

During the first phase of the Schools Council's work (1964–78), projects tended to be large in scale and national in scope. After its reorganization in 1978 with reduced funding, projects were almost all low cost (for example, the Sex Differentiation project had a budget of £15,000 over two years) and local. Moreover, the Schools Council itself was not without problems. Although it was *the* centralized agency for curriculum development, it was firmly committed to pluralism and teachers' professional autonomy. Thus given the different interests represented by the Council's membership, no particular line of curriculum was ever endorsed. Instead, projects were sponsored individually although post-1978 there was an attempt to create thematic programmes (Raggatt 1983). Furthermore, there was always controversy about how effective the Council was in publicizing its activities and promoting project material (Steadman *et al.* 1982). For example, it never overcame the theoretical, cultural and physical distances between the project planners (generally located in university education departments) and the curriculum implementers in the schools.

It was to overcome these problems of distance that the teacher–researcher or 'action research' movement came into being because, as Carr and Kemmis point out (1986: 19) 'the teacher-as-researcher appealed to the profession as an element of its professionalism' and also 'because it affirmed and justified a well-developed sense of professional autonomy and responsibility'. Certainly, teacher-based curriculum development was *de rigueur* at the Schools Council in the last few years of its life.

Meanwhile, in the wider world outside education, the growth of the Civil Rights and women's movements in the USA and in Europe gave rise to new theories of sexual inequality and its relation to other forms of inequality, for instance those of 'race' and social class. These in turn gave impetus to the passing of the Sex Discrimination Act (Home Office 1975) and the Race Relations Act (Home Office 1976) which together provided formal justification for a reappraisal of gender and race-relations in schooling. Thus teachers, parents and school students began to push for changes to the gendered and racialized lives and experiences of school children and their teachers, informed by telling research studies revealing the endemic nature of sexism and racism in classrooms and playgrounds (e.g. Clarricoates 1978; Kelly 1981; Spender 1981).

Despite this burgeoning research on gender (and on class and 'race') during the latter part of the life of the Schools Council, few projects were devoted to these issues though equality topics were incorporated into some of the larger projects, e.g. the Humanities Curriculum project. Significantly where professional practices were challenged on the basis of social bias and discrimination, these views tended to be suppressed. Thus those few projects with an overtly social justice brief whose reports contained criticisms of teacher practices were censored or even blocked altogether. This happened when the project 'Education for a Multiracial Society' attempted to incorporate material which revealed the prevalence of racist attitudes and practices of teachers. Its report which should have appeared in 1978, only came out in a censored form in 1981, blocked by teacher representatives on Council (Troyna and Williams 1986). Certainly, while at the National Foundation of Educational Research at the end of the 1970s, I was involved in putting forward a proposal on gender and schooling which, I was told later, was 'talked down' or rather 'laughed out' by Max Morris, the powerful teacher union leader.

Despite these problems, the Schools Council remained the principal means of promoting curriculum development in the UK. Not surprisingly, therefore, it was also the first national education body to make a public commitment to addressing issues of gender and schooling. As I have written elsewhere (Weiner 1985a), there were several reasons for this development.

First, the Council needed to make a response to a draft resolution from the European Economic Community (EEC) in 1979 'concerning measures to be taken in the field of education to improve the preparation of girls for working life and to promote equality of opportunity for girls and boys in society' (Schools Council 1979). A formal policy statement arising from this EEC request which sought to make a contribution to the elimination of sex-stereotyping in curricula provided the necessary justification and impetus for the later work of the Council in this area.

Second, individual members (often women) of curriculum committees came together with influential officers in the Council to facilitate wider discussion of gender issues spurred on by the developments of feminist ideas outside education. And third, the Equal Opportunities Commission (EOC) approached officers of the Council with an offer of collaboration between the EOC and the Schools Council in the form of a jointly published series of anti-sexist resource books (Eddowes 1983; Harding 1983; Stones 1983; Whyte 1983). Subsequently, the Schools Council made two direct contributions to curriculum development on gender: by establishing its own curriculum initiative, The Schools Council Sex Differentiation project, as mentioned earlier, and by providing extra financial support for an existing project, 'Girls into Science and Technology' (1980–4) based at Manchester University.

At this time, the principal approach taken by curriculum developers to equality issues was similar to that adopted for other curriculum areas. That is, increased teacher education and development would provide the solution to 'bad' practice. It was thus argued that if teachers discriminated between male and female pupils it was either because they were ignorant about the implications of their practice or because they were ill-informed about equal opportunities (a euphemism for women's/feminist issues) (Weiner 1985a). There was a conspicuous failure to recognize that it was often in the interests of, say, male teachers to condone discrimination against female peers and colleagues; and also to understand that redressing power relations between men and women, girls and boys within education might require more fundamental change than was necessary in other curriculum areas.

It followed, then, that the solution to problems of sexism in education were perceived as lying primarily with educators; in the educational remedies of improved professionalism and pedagogy. It was anticipated (naïvely, it seems now) that by promoting consciousness-raising and improved pedagogy, teachers would, voluntarily, adopt non-sexist professional practices. Thus, the failure or rather, inability, to address the inequalities in power relations which clearly underpin sexist practices provided an obstacle to any dramatic achievements. For example, the Sex Differentiation project was cautious about its successes: encouraging the acceptance of gender as a legitimate area of professional development for teachers, creating a national network for those interested in gender issues, and drawing attention to the importance of having 'committed' individuals at senior management level. Certainly, the project's structural links (through the Schools Council) with the wider curriculum development movement ensured that gender issues attracted a wider audience than, perhaps, they would have otherwise received.

Feminist curriculum developments

Meanwhile more consciously *feminist* ideas on curriculum development were taking form. For example, the Girls into Science and Technology project (GIST) was an action research project which aimed at encouraging more girls to continue physical science and technical craft subjects when these became optional at secondary school. Rather than working mainly through those already committed, the project team took the high risk strategy of working closely with the full range of teachers. The main aims were to reduce sex-stereotyping on the part of pupils and teachers, and to promote 'gender-fair' interaction in classrooms, so that girls would feel encouraged to continue with studying science. Not surprisingly, the main difficulty for the GIST team was that of trying to work with teachers (largely male) who were not at all sympathetic to the goals and methods of the project and, who, in many cases, were overtly anti-feminist.

The main drawback . . . was that, by and large, the teachers did not see girls' under-representation as a problem. Nor were they willing to re-examine their own values. Most teachers readily agreed that equality was important, but thought that it already existed, and that residual differences between girls and boys were genetic. Since they did not accept that there was any sex stereotyping in their classrooms, many teachers did not see the problem as theirs, and did not feel motivated to search for solutions.

(Kelly 1985: 139)

Other projects chose to work with teachers already convinced of the need for change – with the intention of creating a 'ripple' effect. In a curriculum-focused intervention designed to challenge the sex-stereotyped occupational choice of both sexes, the Girls and Occupational Choice project opted for collaboration with a small number of participating schools, and with volunteer teachers. However, they found resistances emerging from concepts of good pedagogical practice.

Our intention was to work as equal partners with teachers committed to the overall objectives of the project in the action research process of developing, implementing and evaluating curriculum intervention units. In practice the situation was somewhat different . . . teachers committed to an individual child-centred approach and to coeducation were wary of using gender as a discriminator for differential behaviour towards children, and indeed of giving girls something which they were not giving to the boys.

(Chisholm and Holland 1987: 251–2)

After the demise of the Schools Council in 1982, when local authorities began to take over various commitments to curriculum reform, feminists within pioneer authorities such as the Inner London Education Authority (ILEA) began to encourage equality initiatives at the school level – through policy development, availability of resources and targeted funding. They also concentrated on developing greater coherence of strategy, emphasizing professional development and the need for whole school policy at the same time as addressing, simultaneously, different elements of underachievement and inequality. For example, Minhas working in the ILEA, outlined a rationale for addressing the triple agendas of gender, race and class thus:

A conceptual understanding of racism/sexism and class bias is essential if pitfalls of 'commonsensical explanations' which often perpetuate stereotypes are to be avoided . . . In fact there is no basis in biological difference for the widespread stereotyping and discrimination on the grounds of sex and race. Distinctions are based on society's expectations and support the continuation of inequality. This raises very serious issues of teacher expectations and the assessment of children by teachers.

(Minhas 1986: 3)

In contrast, Hazel Taylor, working in Brent, an outer London authority, argued for a more devolved model of change. She identified gender equality as a democratic right, fundamentally concerned with the power-sharing aspects of democracy and opted for a bottom-up model of change:

A top-down model of change is clearly not appropriate (even if it would be effective); a bottom-up model is harder to support and likely to produce divergence between institutions, but is the model philosophically most acceptable to the nature of the initiative. It is also morally and practically desirable, as it forces acknowledgement of the fact that much of the innovative work, both in defining the problems in providing an education for gender equality, and in developing practice to bring it about, has been and is actually being done by teachers within their schools.

(Taylor 1985: 126)

Thus Taylor argued for schools to be allowed the freedom to develop their own strategies for change, but within a framework of policy requirements and inducements to ensure that they would all be progressing in the desired direction, albeit at different speeds. However, the autonomy of teachers and indeed local authorities was to be the target of a number of government assaults during the 1980s from an increasingly confident Conservative administration as we shall see in the next section.

The impact of government policy changes from the late 1980s

The 1980s signalled a new era of curriculum change and the production of a range of new curriculum discourses, in which the responsibilities of central and local government, of teachers and the state, were continually reformulated and revised. For example, a development early in the decade was the emergence of the 'contractual agreements' in the curriculum change process, as Burchell (1989: 1) describes:

> The key feature of this framework is that the LEA becomes bound to the centrally defined objectives for the initiative through a contract with a government department or agency (DES or MSC) which is acting as sponsor; in return for 'signing the contract' significant extra funds are made available to the LEA.

While providing financial inducement as a means of securing educational change was far from new, what was different in the 1980s was the tightness of the cords which bound the funder and the funded. However, what was interesting, and somewhat confusing about these often explicitly market-orientated schemes, was that equal opportunities was positioned relatively highly within them. I have suggested elsewhere that the main reason for this was in the perceived need for an unsegmented work-force:

> It could be argued that equal opportunities criteria were injected into TVEI because of the perceived need for a free (that is, unsegmented) labour market to serve the interests of the economy. Schooling's 'delivery' of a flexible workforce – undifferentiated by sex (etc.) – would make adaptation to future changes in manufacturing and service industries much more practicable.
>
> (Weiner 1989b: 117)

By the end of the 1980s, however, the educational agenda was again transformed. Prime Minister Thatcher's third electoral success in 1987 accompanied by a large Conservative majority in Parliament enabled her to force through changes that sought to recast and in most cases, roll back, public sector provision. In education, this meant that power was further centralized with the passage of the Educational Reform Act (ERA) in 1988, which included the introduction of the national curriculum and Local Management of Schools (LMS). What became increasingly clear, also, was the government's determination to break with the past and exclude the education professionals from active participation in any new curriculum formulation and change. Interestingly, once

again, Conservative government policy was not entirely antitheti-
cal to the project of redressing gender equality, since the introduction of a national curriculum with the explicit aim of providing all
children with the same curricular experiences appeared, at first
glance, to address feminist demands for a core curriculum.

The national curriculum, government ministers claimed, was to
be founded on principles of accountability and entitlement. It sought
to preserve 'important' subjects such as history that were in danger of disappearance or dilution; it was to bring definition and
order to others, like English, that had become shapeless; and significantly it promised entitlement for all students – girls as well as
boys – to study subjects like science and technology. Thus it aimed
to define, prescribe and make public hitherto semi-articulated
judgements about curriculum content and pupil performance. The
model of curriculum change adopted here was certainly top-down.
It seemed, at first glance, to be highly effective in terms of level of
implementation (say, compared with the performance of Schools
Council projects as we have already seen), but it also attracted
much criticism regarding curriculum-overload, over-prescription
and over-bureaucracy (see Chapter 6 for a fuller discussion).

In terms of impact of government policy on gender curriculum
initiatives, the outlook was uncertain even though there was indication that equal opportunities had a presence in the new curriculum
era. For instance, 'challenging myths, stereotypes and misconcep-
tions' and 'ensuring equal access to the curriculum means real
opportunity to benefit' were cited as two of six cross-curricular
themes covering 'equal opportunities and education for life in a
multicultural society' (NCC 1992: 15). However, the concept of
equality utilized within the national curriculum was extremely weak;
it was more concerned with removing obstacles to pupil progress
than with aiming to change attitudes or challenge discriminatory
practice. Furthermore, the non-statutory status of equal opportunities, as a cross-curricular theme within a highly prescriptive and
inflexible curriculum framework, denoted the fragility of its positioning.

Moreover, interpretations of the term 'equal opportunities' within
the documentation were less than clear, as Shah points out:

> The various guidelines from the Secretary of State to the
> subject working groups include references to issues of gender
> and the needs of ethnic minority children. However, there

appears to be no consensus. In some instances the term equal opportunities refers to the attainment of girls, sometimes to gender differentiation in assessment, in some instances to both boys and girls, and occasionally to ethnic minority pupils. The Technology report puts Special Needs under the general heading of Equal Opportunities.

(Shah 1990: 315)

Moreover, there was also considerable variation between subject areas, as to whether equal opportunities issues needed to be addressed at all. While science and history 'have attempted to be positive', Shah is sharply critical of the mathematics report's hostility to multi-cultural issues as indicative of 'the continued powerful opposition to equality, especially for black people' (Shah 1990: 315).

Simultaneous to the emergence of the national curriculum, earlier advocates of gender reform were under attack at a number of levels. First, the continued ideological hostility of central government to equality issues (and consequent lack of resources) – which had now lasted for more than a decade – made any curriculum initiatives (other then those required by the national curriculum) extremely difficult to sustain. Second, the inability of the much weakened local education authorities to continue to support equality developments had an enormous impact. This loss of support was particularly noticeable in the case of the strong Labour urban administrations such as the Inner London Education Authority (ILEA) which, as we have seen, had mounted significant equality initiatives over the previous decade. Third, the low morale among teachers who had seen their professional status and conditions of service undercut and their local authorities destroyed, meant that they were unlikely to have the enthusiasm or the energy to continue to mount challenges to the educational status quo. Further, though they now had responsibility for making the educational changes work, they were excluded from policy discussions about how this could best be done. The extensive boycotts of national testing arrangements in the early 1990s are illustrative of the extent of teacher alienation at this time. Fourth, the complexity of the arrangements for assessment and monitoring the national curriculum proved to be so bulky and time-consuming that there seemed little opportunity for subversion or for the pursuit of alternative educational agendas.

At the time of writing therefore, belief in state policy as a means of addressing equality (let alone feminist) issues is at an all time low. What is, nevertheless, important to remember is that, alongside current official curriculum discourses which cannot be viewed as other than regressive, interest and commitment to eradicating inequalities in education goes on, as we shall see in the next chapter.

Ways forward

So what can be made of this admittedly selective account of curriculum development? First, it implies legitimation for gender curriculum reform within curriculum discursive frameworks since social advancement is one of the four constant features of curriculum, as mentioned at the beginning of this chapter (the other three are selection, differentiation and functionality). It is particularly important to note that, in a democracy, education has never been concerned only with supplying the needs of the economy or ensuring effective socialization; it also has strong traditions of preparing for citizenship, extending possibilities for learning and promoting social progress.

Second, what is also apparent is that the curriculum itself is necessarily gendered because of its close links with schooling and the state. Historically, as we have seen in education but also in policy on housing, health, welfare benefits etc., state policy has been suffused with sexist assumptions about the needs and potential of individuals. Notions of what constitutes an appropriate education for girls and for boys have differed over time, yet, even well into the mid-1980s, as illustrated by the GIST teachers, physiological or social-conditioning reasons were still offered to explain away discrimination and inequality. In fact, it is hard to avoid the numerous allusions, within the curriculum literature, to the conflicting nature–nurture duality, characterized in terms of the perceived oppositional forces of women's nature on the one hand, and female education on the other.

Third, whilst each of the two most active eras of curriculum development, the 1960s and the 1980s, took off in very different ideological climates, the opportunities for those wishing to promote greater equality in education were not noticeably different. The social democratic or 'professional' ethos of the Schools Council was, perhaps, even less conducive to challenging forms of inequality than the market-driven vocationalism of the 1980s which seemed more in accord with liberal feminist ideas concerning the freedom of girls and women to move up the educational and occupational ladder. As I have written elsewhere:

> Many would argue ... for the professional approach as more appropriate for schooling, both ethically and educationally. Choices are less clear for feminists, however, since the assumptions and behaviour underpinning past professional practices in education have drawn strong criticism ... It could be argued that bureaucratic/vocational policies are more 'girl-friendly' since equal opportunities have been more highly prioritised by them. In contrast, 'professional' approaches have proved highly resistant, although more recently they have accepted feminist analyses as part of the wider education debate.
>
> (Weiner 1989b: 119)

There still remains a main curriculum problem for feminists: how to resolve the tension between the principal organizing curriculum feature of control and order, and the ideological framework of feminism which rests on the commitment to expanding rights and freedom? Perhaps resorting to the notion of a variety of feminisms rather than one unified feminism might be helpful here (for a detailed discussion, see Chapter 4). For example, the curriculum initiatives on gender developed in the 1980s tended to perceive the demands of *liberal feminists* favourably, as synonymous with 'liberal', *laissez-faire* ideas about the need for labour market freedom and the need to create internal markets within education. This has parallels with Dawes' (1992) claim that liberal feminism is in sympathy with 'system maintaining curriculum theories' in that its main orientation is increased access to existing structures and toleration of dominant social values.

On the other hand, more critical feminisms, such as those of *radical or socialist feminists* are more in accord with Dawes' 'system opposing curriculum theories' in their demands for fundamental changes not only in terms of access to educational benefits but more widely to embrace curriculum knowledge and schooling structures. Certainly *poststructural feminism* can offer a clearer analytical framework on which to base future curriculum challenges and counter discourses in its emphasis on agency as well as structure and in its focus on revealing how power is exercised through discourse.

Is there a future for feminism, then, in future curriculum metamorphoses? Whilst this question will be addressed in subsequent chapters, perhaps, first, we need to know what forms of feminisms are available to us, and also why education has appeared relatively resistant to feminist challenges. Thus, discussion of developments within feminism and how they apply to education will form the basis of the next chapter.

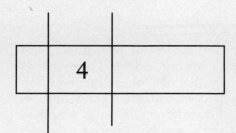

4

Feminisms and education

Introduction

Many people think of feminism as a comparatively recent phenomenon – a rather 'hippy' and utopian vision left over from the
1960s and 1970s. Some have even termed the 1980s onwards as
a 'post-feminist' era in which women can relax at last, safe in the
knowledge that all the necessary gains (the vote, equal pay, opportunities in the labour market, sexual freedom and so on) have
been safely secured (Rumens 1985).

In fact, feminism has a very long history even though the term
is of more recent origin. It derives from the Latin *femina* (woman),
feminism initially meaning 'having the quality of females', and
came into use as a perspective on sexual equality in the 1890s.
Rossi (1974) traced its first usage in print to a book review published in *The Athenaeum*, 27 April 1895 although this does not
signal the beginning of feminism as a movement since, prior to
this 'womanism' was more commonly used to describe interest in
sex equality issues. According to Tuttle (1986: 349), nineteenth-
century usage of the term 'The Woman Question' to denote interest
in the condition of women signalled 'a pre-feminist consciousness'

rather than feminism as a political movement, as it is conceived today. To purloin Dale Spender's book title, indeed, 'There's Always Been a Women's Movement' (Spender 1983b). As feminist historians have found, if you look hard enough, every era has had its share of women complaining of their lot in relation to their male contemporaries. From Sappho in the seventh century BC, through the middle ages to the modern (and even the post-modern) period, there has been a distinctive feminist presence in history.

However, different feminisms have prioritized different aspects of women's struggle against oppressive forces. It has been common in recent years to categorize each feminism according to its particular ideological source in order to show the differences within feminism as well as the shared commitment to women's advancement. In 1987, Madeleine Arnot and I identified three perspectives on feminism which, we argued, had made the most impact on education: these we termed 'Equal Rights in Education' (namely liberal feminism), 'Patriarchal Relations' (radical feminism) and 'Class, Race and Gender: Structures and Ideologies' (marxist/socialist feminism) (Arnot and Weiner 1987). We were later rightly criticized for rendering as marginal those feminisms on the fringes of our three categories, in particular, black feminism and lesbian feminism. Measor and Sikes catalogue four main strands of feminism in their book on gender and schooling – liberal, radical, socialist and psychoanalytic – (Measor and Sikes 1992), while Tong in her introduction to feminist thought published in 1989, distinguishes liberal, marxist, radical, psychoanalytic, socialist, existentialist and postmodern feminisms, seven in all. As poststructuralism rightly identifies, it is proving ever more difficult to categorize the amoeba-like changes in feminism, due to the shifting nature of terminology, say of 'woman' or 'feminism' or 'femininity' and the discursive frameworks which have helped shape the 'normalizing' processes for generations of women. Indeed hooks (1984) argues that feminist thought is always a 'theory in the making', always open to re-examination and new possibilities. Moreover, if there is any agreement about feminism, as Mitchell points out, it is likely to be of a general and diffuse nature.

> If feminism is a concern with issues affecting women, a
> concern to advance women's interests, so that therefore any-
> one who shares this concern is a feminist, whether they

acknowledge it or not, then the range of feminism is general
and its meaning is equally diffuse.

(Mitchell 1986: 12)

However, what has clearly marked out modern feminism has
been its emphasis on the need for feminist *consciousness*; that is,
the concern to understand what has caused women's subordination
in order to campaign and struggle against it. Because such theoretical understandings (of the causes of women's oppression) are
dependent on ideological and political value positions, however,
and also because feminism as 'theory in the making' is resistant
to any one dominant discourse, any attempts to summarize differences in feminist perspective are necessarily hazardous and vulnerable to criticism. Nevertheless, in this chapter I shall attempt
(perhaps unwisely) to consider, as far as it is possible, the various
shifts in modern feminist thought and their impact on education,
at the same time as emphasizing feminism's 'harmonious' goals of
equality and sisterhood, and its discordant tones of difference and
identity.

Feminisms and feminist thought

We tend to be familiar with the two most recent feminist 'waves':
the first, in the nineteenth century stretching into the first two
decades of the twentieth century, and the second, from the late
1960s onwards.

The 'first wave' movement was associated with the emergence
of liberal individualism and Protestantism at the time of the Enlightenment (at the end of the eighteenth and beginning of the
nineteenth centuries), drawing specifically on ideas about natural
rights, justice and democracy. Not surprisingly given its origins,
the movement was *liberal, bourgeois* and highly *individualistic*,
principally concerned with extending legal, political and employment rights of middle-class women. Whilst different class interests
such as Owenites, Chartists, Unitarians and middle-class reform-
ers united in campaigning on 'The Woman Question' (often as
part of a pattern of reforms that embraced universal suffrage and
a national system of education), improvement of the marriage
property laws, greater access to education and the professions,
wider employment opportunities and participation of women in

government and public life undoubtedly yielded greater benefits for middle-class women.

Liberal feminism, which has arguably been the most enduring and accepted of all the feminisms (visible currently in the campaigns in the UK for more women members of parliament and for the rights of women to become Church of England clerics on an equal basis with men) asserts that individual women should be as free as men to determine their social, political and educational roles, and that any laws, traditions and activities that inhibit equal rights and opportunities should be abolished. Access to education is fundamental to this perspective since it claims that by providing equal education for both sexes, an environment would be created in which individual women's (and men's) potential can be encouraged and developed. Liberal feminists also assume that equality for women can be achieved by democratic reforms, without the need for revolutionary changes in economic, political or cultural life, and, in this, their views are in sharp contrast to those of other feminist campaigners.

The 'second wave' women's movement had more dissident origins and aims, although was initially much influenced by the liberal feminism of Betty Friedan whose 1963 publication, *The Feminine Mystique* has been popularly regarded as signalling its beginnings. The Women's Liberation Movement (WLM, also called the modern or new feminist movement) was born in the USA in the 1960s out of other movements of the political 'new' Left, particularly the Civil Rights and anti-Vietnam war movements. A group of women, thoroughly disenchanted with the male domination of political organizations ostensibly committed to democratic/egalitarian practices, began to explore ideas about women-centredness in political organizations and to organize their own autonomous movement for women's liberation. Though its debt to marxism is clearly evident in the terminology used, for example Shulamith Firestone's *Dialectic of Sex* (1970) sought to define society in terms of a sex/class system and offered the case for a feminist revolution, the ideas developed came to be known as those characterizing *radical feminism*.

First, the concept of 'patriarchy' was used to analyse the principles underlying women's oppression. Its original meaning – the rule of the father – was altered to describe the historical dominance of men over women, this being seen as the prototype of all other oppressions and necessary for their continuation.

> Male supremacy is the oldest, most basic form of domina-
> tion. All other forms of exploitation and oppression . . . are
> extensions of male supremacy . . . All men have oppressed
> women.
>
> (*Redstockings Manifesto*, quoted in Bouchier 1983)

Further, Millett (1971) argued that patriarchy is analytically independent of capitalist or other modes of production and Firestone
(1970) defined patriarchy in terms of male control over women's
reproduction.

However, whilst the concept of patriarchy has been crucial to
modern feminism because as Humm (1989: 159) puts it 'feminism
needed a term by which the totality of oppressive and exploitative
relations which affect women could be expressed', different feminist
discourses produce different versions of how patriarchy is constituted, as we shall see later in this chapter.

Another related assumption of radical feminism is that of the
'universal oppression of women'. It necessarily follows that if all
men oppress women, women are *the* oppressed class, though there
has been some disagreement about how patriarchal relations were/
are created and sustained. Firestone (1970) argued that the fundamental inequality between men and women is traceable to the
physical realities of female and male biology (particularly their
roles in reproduction) and their consequences. Ortner (1974) in
contrast, saw the relegation of women to the private sphere arising
out of the *interpretation* of biology in terms of women's association with nature and men's, with culture and civilization.

The third main assumption of radical feminism is that, to be
aware of the effects of male domination, women have to undergo
a process of women-focused education (or re-education) known as
'consciousness raising'. Developed in the 1960s, consciousness
raising is a means of sharing information about female experience
and was used as a means of education for women in the absence
of a comprehensive knowledge-base on women.

> We wanted to get the truth about how women felt, how we
> viewed our lives, what was done to us and how we func-
> tioned in the world. Not how we were *supposed* to feel but
> how we really did feel. This knowledge, gained through honest
> examination of our personal experience, we would pool to
> help us figure how to change the situation of women.
>
> (Shulman 1980: 154)

For a time, during the 1970s, radical feminist goals dominated the 'second-wave' women's movement as it drew in women from a wide range of backgrounds and interests. In Britain, Rowbotham remembers that there seemed to be small groups in most large towns, loosely connected together through national conferences; thus, 'the movement was sufficiently concerted to back national campaigns, for example on abortion' (Rowbotham 1989: xii).

Feminists grouped to address one or more of the numerous concerns of women characterizing the last quarter of the twentieth century: issues such as sexuality, women's health, abortion and reproductive rights, pornography, male violence, and also access to and conditions of employment, child-care provision, sexual harassment in the workplace and so on. The need to create a knowledge-base that illuminated the experiences of women resulted in a burgeoning feminist scholarship and also the emergence, particularly in the United States, of a proliferation of Women's Studies courses. Further, the perceived need to create a more effective, female, political power-base led to increased interest in the development of women-friendly organizations and practices (non-hierarchical, cooperative etc). This was characterized by 'the refusal of formal delegated structures of political organisation, a stress on participation rather than representation' (Mitchell 1986: 26).

Further, as Mitchell (1986) points out, radical feminism not only sought to challenge contemporary sexual relations and politics; it also produced a new language and a new discursive framework based on liberation and collectivism.

> One of the most striking features of women's liberation and radical feminism was their recourse to a new language – the language of liberation rather than emancipation, of collectivism rather than individualism.
>
> (Mitchell 1986: 26)

However, by the end of the 1970s, a number of different feminist perspectives surfaced to challenge the hegemonic position of radical (and to some extent, liberal) feminism, both as a critique and an extension of the feminist project. For example, women within *marxist* and *socialist* organizations began, in a sense, to strike back at the sisters who had originally defected, although in Britain, as early as the 1950s, Juliet Mitchell had begun to articulate feminist ideas within the British Left. Because she was criticized by male comrades for ideological incorrectness, she began to develop a feminist position that demanded changes outside conventional marxist economic and social policy. These included changes in: *production* – women's place in the labour market; *reproduction* – sexual divisions within the family; *sexuality* – in the views of women as primarily sexual beings and sex-objects; and *socialization* – in the way in which the young were reared and educated (Mitchell 1971).

Later, other marxist and socialist feminists attempted to incorporate ideas about women's oppression and patriarchal relations into classic marxism, focusing in particular, on the relationship between production (the labour market) and reproduction (the family); the interrelationship of capitalism and patriarchy; and the complex interplay between gender, culture and society (see, for example, Barrett 1980; Davis 1981; Segal 1987).

Accordingly, patriarchy has a materialist and historical basis in that capitalism is founded on a patriarchal division of labour. Hartmann (1976) for example, defined patriarchy as a set of social relations with a material base underpinned by a system of male hierarchical relations and solidarity.

An important emphasis was that of the impact of class on gender formation exemplified in MacDonald's claim that gender and class are inexorably drawn together within capitalism:

> both class relations and gender relations, while they exist within their own histories, can nevertheless be so closely interwoven that it is theoretically very difficult to draw them apart within specific historic conjunctures. The development of capitalism is one such conjuncture where one finds patriarchal relations of dominance and control over women buttressing the structure of class domination.
>
> (MacDonald 1981: 160)

Whilst this feminist perspective had greater explanatory power, it appeared to be less successful than radical feminism in attracting large numbers of women to its political position, possibly because in seeking to incorporate feminist ideas within marxism, its complexities posed an obstacle to all but the most theoretically sophisticated.

In many ways, the most important challenge to radical feminism came from *black feminism* which criticized not only the white, patriarchal society for triply oppressing black women (on the basis

of sex, colour and class) but also the oppressive nature of the
white women's movement which had glossed over economic and
social differences between women in its attempt to articulate an
authentic, overarching female experience. Moreover, in the United
States, both waves of feminism were associated with black political campaigns: in the nineteenth century, around the abolition of
slavery and in the twentieth, around the Civil Rights movement.
The apparently new black feminist presence was to shatter ir-
reparably the notion of universal sisterhood – though as Tuttle
points out, black feminism has been in existence as long as white
feminism 'although [it has] . . . suffered the fate of most women of
being "lost" to history' (Tuttle 1986: 41).

Black feminists challenged the idea that a feminism that ignores
racism can be meaningful. As bel hooks wrote in 1984:

> Feminist theory would have much to offer if it showed women
> ways in which racism and sexism are immutably connected
> rather than pitting one struggle against the other, or blatantly
> dismissing racism.
>
> (hooks 1984: 52)

Moreover, it mounted a challenge to some of the most central
concepts and assumptions of the white women's movement. Carby
argues, for example, that the concept of 'patriarchy' has different
meanings for black women.

> We can point to no single source of our oppression. When
> white feminists emphasize patriarchy alone, we want to re-
> define the term and make it a more complex concept. Racism
> ensures that black men do not have the same relations to
> patriarchal/capitalist hierarchies as white men.
>
> (Carby 1982, reprinted 1987: 65)

hooks further argued that the concentration of the white feminist
movement on identifying white middle and upper-class men as the
'enemy' and the 'oppressor' let other men off the hook.

> The labeling of the white male patriarch as 'chauvinist pig'
> provided a convenient scapegoat for black male sexists. They
> could join with white and black women to protest against
> white male oppression and divert attention away from their
> sexism, their support of patriarchy and their sexist exploita-
> tion of women.
>
> (hooks 1982, pp. 87–8)

Black feminists pioneered the concept of identity politics, of organizing around a specific oppression, which allowed for both difference and equality to become issues within feminist politics. Hill Collins adds a commitment to a humanist vision in her definition of black feminism as 'a process of self-conscious struggle that empowers women and men to actualize a humanist view of community' (Hill Collins 1990: 39). She also draws on standpoint theory to articulate a specific black woman's position in the political economy, in particular, their ghettoization in domestic work enabling them to see white élites from a position not available to black men.

Interestingly, British black feminists retain stronger links with marxist and socialist feminism than their North American counterparts due to the specific experience of British imperialism and colonialism. For example, Brah and Minhas present their feminist position as follows:

> We start from the position that any discussion [of education] ... must be understood in the context of the complex social and historical processes which account for the subordination of black groups in British society. Social relations between white and black groups in Britain today are set against a background of colonialism and imperialism.
>
> (Brah and Minhas 1985: 14)

In particular, British black feminists emphasized the exploitation and unjust treatment of black immigrants (women and men) from the Caribbean and the Asian subcontinent from the 1950s onwards, for example, concerning overt discrimination such as the use of the 'colour bar' in housing, employment and education (Bryan *et al.* 1985). The state was further viewed as having created new forms of racism (termed 'institutional racism') within the bureaucracies and institutions for which it was responsible; thus 'contemporary racism now needs to be seen as a structural feature of the social system rather than a phenomenon merely of individual prejudice' (Brah and Minhas 1985: 15).

Furthermore, the possibility of making generalizations across all groups derived, say, from theories based on the white family as a site of sexual oppression, was heavily criticized. Phoenix (1987) argues that in the light of the endemic and unremitting racism of British society, the black British family is more likely to be a source of strength and a haven, than a site of oppression for black women.

Simultaneously, radical feminism began to exhibit divisions as breakaways championing a *separatist* feminist position were taken up by the 'new age' philosophies of Mary Daly and her followers on the one hand, and political lesbianism on the other. Mary Daly, in her 1979 volume *Gyn/Ecology* offers a new, metaphysical *spiritual feminism* in which men are depicted as evil and death-loving, parasitical on the energies of good, life-loving women. Daly argued that patriarchy is itself the world's prevailing religion and that women need to withdraw from men in order to create a new, women-centred universe with a new philosophy and theology, and even a new language.

Lesbian feminism, in sharp contrast, took a much more overtly political stand, arguing that lesbianism is not simply a matter of sexual preference or an issue of civil rights but rather a whole way of life combining the personal with the political. The concept of *political lesbianism* was developed as a critique of the ideology and practices of heterosexuality. According to Charlotte Bunch,

> Lesbian-feminist politics is a political critique of the institution and ideology of heterosexuality as a cornerstone of male supremacy. It is an extension of the analysis of sexual politics to an analysis of sexuality itself as an institution. It is a commitment to women as a political group, which is the basis of a political/economic strategy leading to power for women, not just an 'alternative community'.
>
> (quoted in Tuttle 1986: 180–1)

The argument was made that since sexual orientation is a matter of personal preference, lesbianism should not be stigmatized and furthermore, that lesbianism should be made more visible within the women's movement, in history and in society as a whole. Moreover, because political lesbianism constitutes a major challenge to male domination in its commitment to an autonomous, women-centred society, it has a legitimate and central place in any movement which seeks to redress the power balances between the sexes.

Significantly, the more 'radical' feminist groupings were remarkably successful in achieving societal attitudinal change, particularly given their relatively small numbers. Their public campaigns, for instance, concerning the seriousness of rape and the establishment of rape crisis centres, the revelation of hitherto unacknowledged incidence of child sexual abuse and male violence in the family, the establishment of havens for battered wives, and campaigns against pornography as a violation of women's civil rights, all fundamentally affected the societies within which they were active (see, for example, Brownmiller 1975; Dworkin 1981).

Another form of feminism to emerge in the 1970s, drawing to some extent on both marxist and radical feminism but also with its own specific knowledge-base was that of *psychoanalytic feminism*. Its main concern was to place greater emphasis within feminism on how the oppression of women affects their emotional life and their sexuality (as opposed, say, to their employment prospects or position within the family). It argued, for instance, that the roots of women's oppression are deeply embedded in the psyche and that for women to free themselves, an 'interior' (as well as societal) revolution is necessary so that women are able to challenge their own oppression. Extending her earlier ideas on the necessary prerequisites for women's liberation (see earlier in this chapter) Mitchell (1982) continued to articulate her concern about the ideologies underlying women's position, this time taking Freud's theories about the unconscious and the construction of femininity and demonstrating their importance as tools for analysing and challenging patriarchal society.

Criticisms of the phallocentric nature of Freud's work led other feminists into alternative ways of theorizing women's position in the family and in child-rearing. Chodorow, for example, explored mother/daughter relationships. Rejecting the notion that women's universal primary role in child-care could be explained in purely biological or social terms, Chodorow claims that women become mothers because they were themselves mothered by women. In contrast, the fact that men are parented by women psychically reduces their potential for parenting. Women's exclusive mothering, Chodorow asserted:

> creates a psychology of male dominance and fear of women in men. It forms a basis for the division of the social world into unequally valued domestic and public spheres, each the province of a different gender.
>
> (Chodorow 1978)

According to this view, patriarchy stems from the gender formation of females and males, uniting psychic and property relations

(Dinnerstein 1976). Thus to achieve women's liberation, the family must be reorganized so that women and men share parenting responsibilities equally and children grow up dependent upon both women and men from their earliest days. Not surprisingly given other radical feminist perspectives, major criticisms of Chodorow's thesis includes her prioritization of psychic dynamics over social structures in women's liberation, and her failure to appreciate the diversity of family structures inter- and intra-culturally (Tong 1989).

Other, more complex (and often more confusing!) critical feminisms emerged in the 1980s to challenge and critique both the women's movement and patriarchal relations, developing out of the general disillusionment with science and macro-political theory in the post-Chernobyl and post-Communist/Cold War eras. They were grounded, as Lather writes, in 'the disappointed hopes engendered by optimistic confidence in the continuing progress and imminent triumph of Enlightenment reason' (Lather 1991: 87).

They arose out of theories of poststructuralism and postmodernism, increasingly popular and influential in the social sciences towards the end of the 1980s. However, there was much confusion about what poststructuralism and postmodernism brought to the understanding of social relations. In fact, Hudson reveals the extent to which characterizations of postmodernism differ: seen alternatively as a myth, periodization, condition or situation, experience, historical consciousness, sensibility, climate, crisis, episteme, discourse, poetics, retreat, topos, and task or project (Hudson 1989: 140). Calinescu (1985) suggests however that postmodernism is principally used in two ways: as a historical category (namely defining a post-modern era) and as a systematic or ideal concept (namely a theoretical, analytic framework). Also, its relationship to poststructuralism lies in the acceptance by poststructuralists of the analytic framework but not the sense of periodization.

Thus, if postmodernist critiques aim to deconstruct philosophical claims generally, and the very idea of possible unitary theories of knowledge, *post-modern feminism* also concentrates on such critiques but within feminism (Nicholson 1990). Accordingly, feminism is perceived as having much in common with postmodernism in questioning the 'foundationalism and absolutism' (Hekman 1990: 2) of the modern historical period (from the late eighteenth century onwards); in criticizing the claims to objectivity and rationality of modern (male) western scholarship; and in asserting that this epistemology must be displaced and a different way of describing human knowledge and its acquisition must be found.

> Feminism, like postmodernism, poses a challenge to modern thought in every discipline from philosophy to physics, but the cutting edge of both critiques is to be in those disciplines that study 'man'. Both feminism and postmodernism are especially concerned to challenge one of the defining characteristics of modernism, the anthropocentric [male-centred] definition of knowledge.
>
> (Hekman 1990: 1–2)

However, Hekman makes the point that feminism is also tied to the universalisms of Enlightenment epistemology, both because of its modernist legacy (namely the emergence at the end of the eighteenth century of liberal feminism as part of Enlightenment thinking in, say, the work of Mary Wollstonecraft, 1792), and because of radical feminism's adherence to dichotomies and absolutes connected with revealing an essential nature of womanhood. Accordingly, a post-modern approach to feminism must necessarily reject outright the epistemological categories that have created and sustained the female–male dualism and also aim to reveal some of the flaws in contemporary feminism, such as the attempt to define an essential female nature (such as by Mary Daly), the failure to recognize the historical and cultural embeddedness of its own assumptions, or to replace the current 'masculinist' epistemology with a similarly flawed 'feminine-ist' epistemology. Moreover, if all knowledge (including that created by feminism) is perceived as interpretive and open to criticism this will add considerable substance and power to the overall feminist critique.

In contrast, *poststructural feminism* has placed more emphasis on the creation of new ways of seeing and knowing. Drawing on the work of the French philosopher Michel Foucault among others, poststructural *feminism* seeks to analyse in more detail the workings of patriarchy in all its manifestations – ideological, institutional, organizational and subjective. Moving away from the universals of liberal and radical feminism, social relations are viewed in terms of plurality and diversity rather than unity and consensus, enabling an articulation of alternative, more effective ways of thinking about or acting on issues of gender (Wallach Scott 1990).

A poststructural analysis, it is argued, differs fundamentally from structuralist analyses such as that of the linguist Saussure in that it recognizes the importance of 'agency' as well as structures in the production of social practices:

> It recognizes not only the constitutive force of discourse and the social structures emerging through those discourses, but accords the possibility of *agency* to the subject. For children and anyone else not accorded full human status within society, agency stems from a critical awareness of the constitutive force of discourse.
>
> (Davies and Banks 1992: 3)

Thus people are not socialized into their personal worlds, not passively shaped by others but rather, each is active in taking up discourses through which he or she is shaped.

Moreover, feminist poststructuralism argues that what it means to be a 'woman' and/or to be acceptably 'feminine' shifts and changes as a consequence of discursive shifts and changes in culture and history. If the meanings of concepts such as 'womanhood' or feminism, for that matter, are necessarily unstable and open to contestation and redefinition, then they require continual scrutiny; according to Wallach Scott (1988: 5):

> they require vigilant repetition, reassertion and implementation by those who have endorsed one or another definition. Instead of attributing transparent and shared meaning to cultural concepts, poststructuralists insist that meanings are not fixed in a culture's lexicon but are rather dynamic, always potentially in flux.

What poststructural feminism claims to be able to do, then, even if it lacks any substantive powerbase, is to offer discursive space in which the individual woman is able to resist her subject positioning (a specific fixing of identity and meaning). According to Weedon (1987: 105):

> A constant battle is being waged for the subjectivity of every individual – a battle in which real interests are at stake, for example, gender-based social power – dominant, liberal-humanist assumptions about subjectivity mask the struggle.

As a 'reverse-discourse', feminism is positioned to challenge meaning and power, enabling the production of new, resistant discourses. Weedon suggests, however, that radical feminism has failed to do this thus far since it has run parallel to the hegemonic, male discourse, rather than subverting its power. On the other hand, while privileging the interests of women, feminist poststructuralism, Weedon argues, is more analytical and illuminating in revealing how power is exercised through discourse, how oppression works and how resistances might be possible.

Criticisms of postmodernism and poststructuralism have largely been concerned with questioning their appropriateness, although theoretically strong, for political action. Thus the charge that postmodernist (and indeed poststructuralist) feminism cannot provide a viable political programme because it rejects absolute values and verges on relativism, needs seriously to be addressed even though its rejection of male-defined knowledge and action is one of the most obvious goals of feminism.

The range of feminisms described above, I suggest, are those that have been of most influence to British feminism; however, other forms have had greater prominence in other cultures. In France, for example, different forms of feminism have emerged both out of *existentialism* and *poststructuralism/postmodernism* – indeed Tong claims that until recently, post-modern feminism was popularly referred to as 'French feminism' (1989: 217).

In the first instance, drawing on the work of the French existential philosopher Jean-Paul Sartre in her 1949 book *Le Deuxième Sexe*, Simone de Beauvoir (1953) conceptualized woman's oppression as unique, derived from her position as the Other, not only separate from man but inferior to him. Her perception of the effects on women of having and caring for children suggested to de Beauvoir that it was harder for a woman to become and remain 'a self', especially as a mother. Writing at a time when feminism was at a low point, de Beauvoir argued the case for cultural factors in women's oppression, seeing causes and reasons beyond those suggested by female biology and physiology to account for why woman is invariably selected by society to play the role of the Other (de Beauvoir 1953). At the time of writing *Le Deuxième Sexe*, de Beauvoir declared that she was not a feminist, believing the class struggle to be more important and that women's rights would come with the achievement of socialism. In the 1970s, however, she joined the Women's Liberation Movement, latterly convinced of the need for women to unite to fight against the manifest continuation of sexual inequality in revolutionary, leftist societies.

Later, in the 1980s, younger French feminist writers such as

Cixous, Irigaray and Kristeva drew on the work of de Beauvoir as well as the philosophical writings of Foucault, Derrida and Lacan, to develop a philosophy of *deconstructionism* which aims to illuminate the internal contradictions of the predominant systems of thought and also to reinterpret Freudian psychoanalytic theory and practice (Tong 1989). Cixous (Cixous 1971), for instance, applies Derrida's notion of 'differance' to writing, contrasting feminine writing (*l'écriture feminine*) with masculine writing (*literatur*) and arguing that these differences are psychically constructed. For a variety of socio-cultural reasons, masculine writing has reigned supreme over feminine writing with the consequence that man has been associated with 'all that is active, cultural, light, high or generally positive and women with all that is passive, natural, dark, low or generally negative' (Tong 1989: 224). However, the legacy of de Beauvoir is also clearly evident in this strand of French feminist thought since Cixous also asserts that man is the self and woman is his Other; and woman exists in man's world on his terms. She further argues that women need to write themselves out of the world men have constructed for them by putting into words the unthinkable/unthought, and by using women's own particular forms of writing.

As feminism has become more fractured, and identity politics more possible, other feminisms have continued to emerge: for example, *Christian feminism* (concerned with the creation of a feminist theology – e.g. Maitland 1983) *humanist feminism* (advocating equality that judges women and men by a single standard – e.g. Young 1985); *Muslim feminism* (which sees women's liberation as both more threatening to Islam than it is in the West but also more broadly based – e.g. Mernissi 1985); *eco-feminism* (another broadly-based movement with aims ranging from a quest for a new spiritual relationship with nature to concern to empower women in developing countries – e.g. Vidal 1993) and so on. Conflicts within feminism led also to the use of labels of a more derogatory nature for the activities and beliefs of certain forms of feminism by those holding alternative views: for example, the terms 'revisionist', 'bourgeois', 'career' have all been applied to liberal feminism (Tuttle 1986) which has often been viewed by more radical feminist perspectives as conservative and conformist.

If anything is certain, it is that new feminisms will continue to emerge in the decades to come to reflect the different cultural, psychological and material concerns of new generations of women, rather than any terminal decline of feminism or entry into any post-feminist era.

Feminisms and education

Having attempted, albeit briefly, to give a flavour of the variety of feminisms that have influenced British culture, I want now to pay some attention to how these influences have permeated education. In particular, I shall evaluate their impact on *educational research* and the issues that feminists have chosen to research and the implications of their findings; and *educational understanding* concerning the explanations, causes and effects, given by feminists for the inequalities that currently exist between the sexes in schools.

Feminisms and educational research

It will come as no surprise that different feminist perspectives have generated different research questions for education. For example liberal feminist research studies have tended to focus on girls' 'failure' or underachievement in the schooling system and education more generally in order to campaign for change. They have thus explored the apparent failure to achieve by girls and young women at school, in higher education and in the workplace in relation to their male peers; the causes of differential attainment patterns between the sexes in certain subject areas (particularly in maths, science and technology); sex-stereotyping in optional subject areas and in careers advice; bias in the way examinations and tests are constructed and marked; sex-differences in school staffing patterns, and so on. The aim has been very clearly directed towards working within the current system to achieve change quickly and with minimal disruption. Thus, in utilizing terms such as access, choice, disadvantage, underrepresentation and underachievement, a discourse is produced in which the most acceptable answers are those that are unlikely to make too many overtly threatening demands on a largely sceptical (and male) educational status quo.

Radical feminists within education, on the other hand, seem to have no such reservations about alienating the educational establishment, being concerned with more fundamental criticisms of the male domination of society and the nature of school knowledge. Thus their research questions have tended to focus on critiquing 'male' school subjects, and examining the patriarchal processes of schooling and power relations between the sexes in the classroom. Unlike their liberal feminist sisters, they prioritize the role played by sexuality in the oppression of girls and women in the classroom and staffroom, and in the schooling process more generally. A key debate has been whether there is a role for the single-sex school in the creation of an autonomous female learning culture (see Deem 1984, for a full discussion of this). Thus, the terms most frequently used within this feminist research discourse – patriarchal relations, domination and subordination, oppression and empowerment, woman and girl-centredness – signal both its connectedness to radical feminist thinking in general and its fundamental criticism of current educational practice.

Alternatively, marxist and socialist feminist research on education appears more complex in orientation, concerned with examining the degree to which education and schooling have been effective in producing sexual inequality, say compared, to the reproduction of class inequality. In particular, researchers have focused on how gender and power relations are continually reproduced in schooling (Clarricoates 1978; Wolpe 1988); the formation of gendered class groupings in the schooling context, namely the process by which working-class girls and boys become working-class women and men (Willis 1977; McRobbie 1978); and the relationship between the family, schooling and the labour market in maintaining dominant class and gender relationships (David 1980; Griffin 1985). The concepts utilized within this discourse – capitalism, production, reproduction, class, gender, patriarchal relations, correspondence theory etc. – are distinctively marxist in origin, insightful in pointing up the different positioning of pupils within state (and private) schooling. Yet it is not a discourse that has been influential for practitioners in the classroom, yielding little ground to general feminist demands for accessibility in theorizing for, as well as about, women.

As previously stated, black feminists also mounted a vigorous attack on schooling, criticizing in particular the endemic nature of both racism and sexism. Rather than focusing on the 'clash of cultures' explanations given by many white teachers for the general underperformance of black girls and young women (Brah and Minhas 1985), they concentrated on exposing the pathologization of black family culture and fracturing the widely held stereotypes of black femininity. They explored, for instance, the *actual* experience of black girls and young women in British schooling and in higher education (Amos and Parmar 1984; Mirza 1992); the sexism and racism of teachers (Wright 1987); and the simultaneous construction of women and black students as a problem for, and within, education (Williams 1987). The terminology of this discourse – for example, antisexism, antiracism, black disadvantage, institutional racism, stereotyping, lack of expectation – seems more eclectic in origin than those of other feminist positions drawing on discourses from antiracism as well as from the variety of feminist discourses available.

Other feminisms appear to have had less impact although poststructuralism has recently been more influential. Jones suggests that in contrast to feminist macro-theories of education, feminist poststructuralism holds to a view of 'positive uncertainty' (Jones 1993: 158) in which complexity rather than pattern prevails:

> When girls are seen as multiply located, and not unambiguously powerless, a feminist approach to classroom research must shift away from the 'disadvantage' focus. An interest in the *unevenness* of power means that ... studies might focus on the ways in which girls are *variously* positioned in the classroom.
>
> (Jones 1993: 160–1)

One of the key proponents of this form of analysis, Walkerdine, explores the ideology of progressive pedagogy which although conceived in terms of the liberation of children, she sees as clearly oppositional to the liberation of female teachers (Walkerdine 1990). Accordingly, the 'regime of truth' of the progressive primary classroom is the male-as-norm child as active and the female-as-norm teacher as passive. The independence and autonomy of the teacher are sacrificed, through her role as quasi-mother, to observing and facilitating the 'naturally' developing activity of the child. At the same time, the working-class, female child or black child is seen as somewhat of a problem since she (he/she) rarely conforms to the ideal child. Thus, according to Walkerdine, in the 'fiction' of the progressive classroom – of freedom, democracy, safety and nature – there is a denial of power and of inequality; the discourse simply does not allow for them to be considered.

Davies' (1989) study of the ways in which sex and gender are constituted through discursive practices fleshes out some of Walkerdine's ideas. Davies looked at story lines and narratives and the ways in which gendered identities are implicated in pre-school children's understandings of the dominant cultural storylines made available to them. She found that children could not necessarily understand feminist stories because their 'hearings' were shaped and informed by dominant, 'regulative' discourses of gender of the traditional children's story or fairy tale.

Lather (1991), more interested in postmodernism as well as poststructuralism, identifies her research aims in terms of 'praxis' and 'self-reflexivity' of the feminist researcher, calling for the displacement of hierarchies as the ordering principle of research.

> The goal is difference without opposition and a shift from a romantic view of the self as unchanging, authentic essence to a concept of the 'self' as a conjunction of diverse social practices produced and positioned socially, without an underlying essence.
>
> (Lather 1991: 82)

She argues, drawing on the experience of a three-year investigation into student resistance to the 'liberatory curriculum' of an introductory women's studies course, that researchers must constantly think against themselves as they 'struggle towards ways of knowing which can move us beyond ourselves' (Lather 1991: 83).

The terminology of this feminist research perspective is, like that of marxist feminism, sometimes highly complex and 'difficult', utilizing terminology such as discourse, subjectivity, power–knowledge, drawn from mainstream postmodernist and poststructuralist writing. In my view, McWilliam (1993) is rightly critical of what she terms the PMT (postmodernist tension) of such writers as Lather who on the one hand, argue for openness and self-reflexivity, yet in using highly complicated writing styles, seem implicitly to deny that possibility to their readers. As McWilliam suggests, 'it is not that there is nothing worthy here . . . the difficulty is that one doesn't so much read this text as wrestle with it' (McWilliam 1993: 201).

Feminisms and educational understanding

Once again, different explanations have been given for why sexual inequalities have continued to cast their shadow on schooling and education more generally. Also, different analyses have generated different solutions and strategies for change. Liberal feminists (such

as those at the Schools Council mentioned in Chapter 3) argue
that ignorance is the main cause of sexual inequality and therefore
knowledge dissemination is the principal solution. In this view,
because sexual inequality within schooling is caused by a variety
of factors such as prejudice (of parents, teachers and society in
general), 'traditional' values, the lack of proper role models and
structural barriers, the solution is twofold: awareness-raising
through in-service training and school/LEA policy-making, and
the removal of the barriers, where necessary, through the use of
law (e.g. by passing equal opportunities legislation).

Radical feminist educators, as might be expected, attribute inequalities in schooling to patriarchal forces and male-dominated
power relationships in which (hetero) sexuality and hierarchy
combine to create the dominant male and subordinate female
dualism. Further, they assert that these are manifested at every
level of society: in the family, in the school, in higher education
and in the workplace. Therefore neither the responsibility nor
solution to sexual inequality can be placed entirely on the shoul-
ders of educators; rather they must do what they can to re-educate
society into non-sexist behaviours and practices, as part of the
overall feminist challenge to patriarchal forces. This view holds
that education can be potentially liberating but not in its present
state; it can only be transformative if it shifts the curriculum, and
school knowledge and educational culture from its male baseline.

Radical feminism has also sought to clarify the nature of patriarchal relations of schooling, looking in particular at the links
between male power, sexual violence, masculinity and femininity,
and sexuality in the context of education. Interestingly, in recent
years it has highlighted the problem of male sexuality.

> Male sexual violence . . . is central to the maintenance of male
> power by being structured into a model of masculinity which
> schools have done little to challenge. But if we are seriously
> committed to equality, then we have to make rather fewer
> curriculum analyses of girls studying physics and boys
> parentcraft and spend rather more time addressing these much
> more difficult issues.
>
> (Jones and Mahony 1989: xv)

The critique underpinning this position – of the heterosexual
normalization within schooling that confirms girls and women in
their subordinate status as properly feminine – constitutes a sharply

focused and, in my view, illuminating analysis of the male–female dualism and the role of the patriarchal state in closing down the options of women. The hope expressed is that of widening opportunities for young people by: 'exposing the lack of safety for girls in many of our schools and . . . placing the often neglected story of sexuality and the social control of girls in education, on the map' (Jones and Mahony 1989: xvi).

Marxist and socialist feminist educators appear to have less faith in the role of education in social change; rather they see it as one of the terrains upon which the sex as well as the class struggle is played out and in which patterns of social domination and subordination are reproduced and sustained. They argue, for example, that working-class girls are doubly disadvantaged in schools in undergoing similar experiences of class inequality to their male peers yet also receiving messages about female inferiority. The solution of this feminist perspective to educational inequality is, thus, fairly limited because of the perceived structural nature of sexual inequality within capitalism (although socialist feminism places equal importance on the influence and necessary overthrow of patriarchy). Nevertheless it has been active in the teacher unions in particular, seeking to challenge the domination of male hierarchies and to place feminist issues on the union agenda (Rowbotham 1989).

Black feminism has also seemed equally sceptical about the extent to which British education can overturn or transform inequalities in society; the law has to some extent been more important in eradicating some of the most overt forms of racial and sexual discrimination. However, black activists have been prepared to point out patterns of institutionalized and individual racism in an effort to re-educate ideologically more sympathetic colleagues into more consciously egalitarian practices. Black feminists have also pointed out that by distinguishing between gender and 'race' issues in education (rather than fusing them) black girls have been effectively rendered invisible. Also, the tendency to treat girls from a variety of ethnic groups as a homogenous group on account of their colour, has been heavily criticized; whilst their encounters with racism might be similar, their often diverse cultural, economic and perhaps religious backgrounds mean that their perception and experience of education is likely to be substantially different.

Postmodernist and poststructuralist feminist educators, although comparatively new on the educational scene, are also beginning to have more to say about inequalities in schooling and about how challenges can be made. Because of their interest in the way in which discourse operates as a 'normalizing' and 'naturalizing' process in which knowledge and power are connected and, also, in their prioritization of the 'local', they argue that it is possible to create a counter-discourse in which the unsayable may be said. One point of action is to promote in students a critical awareness of their positioning within educational discourses. Another is to be alert to possibilities for feminist action as they occur – to be 'street-wise' or to 'get smart' as Lather (1991) puts it. A major problem, however, has been how to create critical consciousness without implying an ideological correctness or clashing with the complex subjectivities and loyalties of female (and male) students.

In this chapter, I have tried to provide a broad overview of the shades and projects of contemporary feminism, in particular as they have influenced educational ideas and practices. If such analyses might be construed as divisive and therefore weakening to the overall feminist project, I suggest that such criticisms are over-timid. It is my contention that feminism must subject itself to the same forms of scrutiny that it applies to other discursive and epistemological frameworks, that it needs to recognize its own embeddedness in history and culture and also that it must come to terms with the inevitability of its splintered existence.

The next chapter will show, in more detail, how these feminisms, particularly those of liberal and radical feminism, have permeated and influenced the British school curriculum and educational practices more generally.

5

Eradicating inequality: feminist practitioners and educational change

This chapter assesses the work that has been carried out in schools by practitioners, and how it has been affected by the policies of various governments. I want to focus, first, on the early achievements (and difficulties) of feminist teachers and activists within education because, as I mentioned in the introduction to this book, their experiences and successes seem in danger either of being written off as 'irrelevant' to the present educational era or forgotten as new feminist initiatives get under way to deal with new circumstances and new contexts of inequality. Thus my aim is to describe and discuss what I consider to be feminists' most significant work in education over the last 15 years in the UK, and also to explore the main theoretical frameworks which informed it, including recent more managerial perspectives.

The second (shorter) part of this chapter explores how we can understand the role of government and the state in gender policy-making, particularly since, with the onset of the round of government reform signalled by the 1988 Education Reform Act, we (in the UK) have been sharply reminded of the capacity for state intervention into every aspect of education from the loftiest pronouncements on policy changes to the day-to-day life of the classroom.

In the final section, I return to re-consider the position of feminist practitioners in education currently. Again, as in previous chapters, I take a generally chronological approach in my discussion of both practitioner and state initiatives to provide a historical and cultural context for the discussion rather than to imply any ordered pattern or progress.

In fact, there have been several key partners in the construction of a discourse on gender policy-making in the UK. Despite the British government's generally muted response to equality issues since 1979, certain state-funded projects such as the Technical and Vocational Educational Initiative (TVEI) have generated some exploration of gender issues and modest changes to curriculum structures (Millman and Weiner 1987; Weiner 1989b). Unquestionably, pioneer local authorities such as the Inner London Education Authority (ILEA), Brent, Ealing and Haringey, were significant both in their support of equality initiatives through policy development, availability of resources and targeted funding, and acceptance of sex-equality as a legitimate professional development issue for teachers (ILEA 1986a,b). Nevertheless, it is my view that it was feminist teachers who made the most notable contribution, first by articulating the need for changes in the sexist (and racist) practices of schools in the late 1970s, and then by preparing the ground and developing the strategies and detail of anti-sexist programmes and practices. The fact that they took principal responsibility for the 'delivery' of equal opportunities, once changes had been agreed upon and also endured backlash and harassment from less 'conscious' colleagues is illustrative of their central positioning in the gender-policy process.

The work of the practitioners

Teachers first began to play a role in the gender policy-making process in their exploitation of new educational discourses of sex equality which were produced as a consequence of the inclusion of education in the Sex Discrimination Act (Home Office 1975). According to Arnot (1987), their role was particularly important after 1979 when the new Conservative administration's perspective on equality (and therefore on promoting sex equality in education) was revealed as being distinctly unenthusiastic. It was left to committed (namely feminist) teachers to force the pace by initiating their own campaigns and projects and by putting pressure on local authorities and teacher unions to provide support for equal opportunities work.

In attempting to gain a broader theoretical framework for their feminism, they focused on feminist issues in their individual studies for higher degree dissertations and theses (see for example, Adler *et al.* 1993) enabling them also to establish extensive and enduring feminist networks across education sectors. By these actions, the feminist commitment to action and challenge in education was nurtured and sustained during the lean years of the market-led ideologies of Thatcherism and still exists as a significant influence on education today.

Also during the 1980s, feminist practitioners acquired a wide range of knowledges, strategies and understandings which helped them mount forceful challenges to schooling (and also to combine their work with those in other areas of inequality such as 'race' and special needs). In considering and analysing the range of teacher strategies, projects and initiatives of such 'pioneer' teachers, a number of areas of interest and activity were discernible.

The first sought to *problematize* gender as an educational issue in order to attract the attention of policy-makers. Taking this stance, feminist teachers aimed to persuade their colleagues (and employers) that educational inequality between the sexes was of mainstream educational concern (Cornbleet and Libovitch 1983). If the Sex Discrimination Act was an official signal to create a more equal society, what, they asked, were schools doing to implement the spirit of the legislation? Also, how could they get issues of gender discussed more seriously in staffrooms? An early strategy was to provide evidence (to 'prove') that inequalities existed in schooling – to put on record 'the hard facts of inequality' (Yates 1985). So, in common with feminist educational researchers as described in Chapter 4, feminist teachers reported on unequal school staffing patterns, sex stereotyping in texts and reading schemes, sex-specific patterns of subject choice at 13-plus, the unacceptability of traditional vocational and career choices and so on. For example, Cornbleet and Libovitch describe the aims of one of the first school working groups on gender established in a north London secondary school at the end of the 1970s as follows:

The working party undertook to examine the effects of sexism in the classroom and throughout the school. This involved studying the sex-stereotyped option choices pupils were taking up, the provision made for pupils outside usual school time, the position of women teachers on the staff in relation to the men teachers, and the problem of unequal teacher time and attention being given to boys at the expense of the girls.

(Cornbleet and Libovitch 1983: 145)

Teachers also focused on the covert influences embedded in what was termed the 'hidden curriculum', particularly concerning teacher attitudes. Thus they assembled and disseminated research findings which revealed that girls were seriously disadvantaged in schooling processes – despite teachers' articulated belief that they treated boys and girls without prejudice (Clarricoates 1978; Spender 1980; Kelly 1981; Stanworth 1981). Emphasis was also placed on the increased probability of women entering the labour force, particularly on the statistical unlikelihood of women remaining in the home for much of their adult lives (Avent 1982).

Once the 'problem' of gender inequality had been established as an issue of professional concern, immediate *change strategies* or solutions were called for; strategies that could be readily injected into school life without too much overall disruption to the general working of schools. A wide variety of strategies were tried out including:

- revising school texts, reading schemes, examination questions and display materials;
- rearranging timetables to enable pupils to opt more easily for non-traditional subjects such as physics for girls and modern languages for boys;
- encouraging wider career aspiration by inviting people in non-traditional jobs into school and developing non-discriminatory careers literature;
- changing school organization by, for instance, 'de-sexing' registers and 'uni-sexing' the school uniform.
- appointing female senior staff as a means of providing positive role models for female pupils;
- establishing equal opportunities working parties and posts of responsibility.

Moreover, there was considerable diversity in the strategies suggested and adopted. At this time, the main focus for teachers (as opposed to academics and researchers) was on *practical* change; how could they help reduce inequalities between the sexes by changing their own and their colleagues' perceptions and practice. As Ord and Quigley argue, such aspirations were perilously balanced:

> Change involves an uneasy balance between conflict and consensus – between moving too fast or too slow, between taking people with you or leaving them stranded and antagonistic ... Do we concentrate on formulating whole school policies or focus on small, sometimes trivial issues? When do we take on the more contentious issues, for example, sexual harassment or male disciplinary procedures, registers in alphabetical order or girls wearing trousers all year. (Though having said this we are aware that in some schools all anti-sexist issues are 'hot'.)
>
> (Ord and Quigley 1985: 104, 105)

Yet the variation in teacher action did not stem merely from local or individual priorities, or from availability of resources and support. They were also based on critical differences in the feminist perspectives of the teachers themselves. Thus, by the early 1980s a third stage was signalled by the appearance of *different feminist teacher perspectives* to challenge sexist practices in education. Although the various feminisms described in Chapter 4 were all visible to some extent during this period, two discourses predominated: the 'equal opportunities' perspective drew on ideas and strategies within liberal feminism, and the 'anti-sexist' or 'girl-centred' perspective, on ideas and strategies from radical feminism. There has been a full discussion about this classification elsewhere (Weiner 1985b, 1986) and as we shall see, other feminisms became more influential later on. However, for the purposes of this chapter, I offer the following brief summary of the perceived differences between the two approaches. 'Equal opportunities' strategies aimed at reforms on behalf of girls and women (and sometimes boys and men) within the existing educational structure whilst 'anti-sexist' approaches endeavoured to challenge unequal power relations between the sexes – as a means of transforming the patriarchal practices within school structures and curricula.

These differences became more visible in the tactics chosen to generate change. The first group placed emphasis on reform from the 'inside': by persuading girls to go into science, reviewing textbooks, developing a common curriculum and changing sex-stereotyped option choices. It also stressed the need for equal female representation in the higher tiers of school – at headship and senior management levels. Those proposing 'girl-centred' educational practices, on the other hand, emphasized more fundamental concerns in their reappraisal of patriarchal relations within schooling, being particularly critical of the dominance of male values and knowledge within curriculum content. What antisexists demanded instead was an epistemological shift in curriculum practices which allowed for *her*story as well as history, promoted girl-centred science in place of conventional science curriculum and put an end to the male domination of curricula, classrooms and schools as a whole.

Drawing on debates and campaigns within radical feminism (as outlined in Chapter 4) they also directed attention to what were perceived as more 'contentious' issues relating to the education of girls and women, such as sexuality, sexual harassment, hetero-sexuality and homophobia. Their stated concern was that of *empowering* female pupils and teachers in contrast to the more moderate aim of the first group, which was for a stronger female presence and *representation* in education. While both wanted to improve educational opportunities for girls and women, those wishing to extend 'equal opportunities' placed greatest emphasis on the need for consensual change through professional development, for example, by demanding increased in-service training as a means of ensuring recognition of sex equality as a professional issue. Alternatively, those advocating antisexist approaches argued for the need both to address the conflicting interests of women and men, and for structural change in order to achieve meaningful progress. Hence they sought to challenge male domination of schooling by, for instance, establishing female support groups and networks, designing girl and women-centred curricula and replacing the perceived male organizational characteristics of hierarchy, competition and managerialism with the more women-identified practices of valuing personal experience, cooperation and democracy. As Spender argued,

By emphasizing the role that the personal plays in learning, feminists have developed an educational paradigm which is sometimes diametrically opposed to the patriarchal one (where

the personal is seen as a source of contamination and the
subjective, something to be avoided).

(Spender 1987: 151)

Although I have used this dual classification of feminist practitioners to explain why certain strategies for change appeared more
attractive to some feminists than others, some critics (e.g. Acker
1986) point to the difficulty, in practice, of identifying such clear
differences in perspective and strategy.

Radical and socialist feminists *do* work within education to
improve the quality of girls' experiences, whatever their
theories say about structures. And some liberals advance
strategies of 'positive action', by which they mean giving
special attention to girls.

(Acker 1986: 67–8)

There was certainly evidence, for example, in the activities of
feminist teacher groups such as the Manchester Women and Education Group and the London-based WedG, that despite theoretical disagreements teachers from a variety of feminist persuasions
were prepared to form alliances in order to strengthen the overall
feminist challenge to education. Thus the Manchester newsletter
of winter 1982 includes articles on science in Soviet schools, nursery provision, the new Youth Training Scheme and the Girls into
Science and Technology project, while the October 1983 WedG
newsletter contains sections on resources and information centres,
theatre groups, teachers' groups, school initiatives and local
authority developments (Women in Education 1982; WedG 1983).
The crusading metaphors of the WedG editorial are indicative of
the prevailing radical feminist discourse within education in the
metropolitan areas at this time.

Major battles are still being fought in schools throughout
London over such fundamental issues as boy/girl segregation
on registers . . . The time and energy being expended on such
issues is an indication of how much needs to be done to
make anti-sexist education a reality.

(WedG 1983: 1)

By the mid-1980s, moreover, differences between activists began
to diminish: first, because the increasing conservatism of government created the need for better organized responses from feminist

teachers (in what was perceived as a divide-and-rule government ethos); and second, because new tactics were developed which both combined the strengths of the various feminist perspectives and drew on their multiplicity of theoretical and practitioner understandings. Thus the aim was to develop more *coherence* whereby some of the more structural demands underpinning antisexist approaches were utilized and integrated within equal opportunities work, less for revolutionary change than for feasible and practical reform. Connections were also made between gender, race and class as black feminism began to make an impact on education:

> Relationships between race, sex and class are dynamic and complex and have implications for classroom practice. If race, gender and class issues are compartmentalized, the teaching approaches and strategies developed for combating racism, sexism and class bias will be limited and less effective than they might be.
>
> (Minhas 1986: 3)

Teachers began to promote policies which addressed racism and sexism across the curriculum, for instance, by focusing on girls' reported experiences of racism in school as a basis for promoting change, and by designing a variety of activities for girls focused on the specifics of their ethnic group membership. Mohamed (ILEA 1986a) describes the aims of a whole school project on Africa in a London primary school.

> We aimed to challenge stereotypical views, show the links between Africa and the Caribbean and link in with the Schools for Africa project and the Band Aid appeal . . . We invited storytellers, musicians, parents and local learning support groups, all of whom contributed enormously to the project . . . The children discussed issues of inequality, raised initially by reading relevant extracts from writing by black women.
>
> (Mohamed 1986: 8)

Issues around sexuality were also prioritized such that hitherto taboo subjects were given a place in policy-making and the curriculum. Some education authorities, as Holly (1989) reports, tried to raise issues about the heterosexual environment of schools by bringing out policy documents that were circulated in schools.

However responses were sometimes extremely hostile, particularly when future policy initiatives involved allowing gay and lesbian teachers to talk openly about sexual choice and orientation. Less contentious strategies included organized conferences and work-shops dealing with assertiveness and confidence training, sexual harassment, sexism, and sexuality for older secondary pupils. Dibb (ILEA 1986b) describes a sixth form conference which included sessions on sexism, sexual harassment, contraception and abor-tion, and 'normality' and sexual orientation. 'We regard these issues', Dibb explains, 'as inextricably linked and believe that in Equal Opportunities we should embrace all areas of discrimination' (ILEA 1986b).

Teachers also began to develop broader strategies for change that depended on simultaneously challenging different areas of schooling. These included: changing the content of curriculum areas, for example, in history, social studies, science, religious education; making science, computing, technical subjects and mathematics more accessible to girls; exploring school policy on general or-ganization and classroom management; developing equal opportu-nities policies in boys' schools; and developing school policy on language, and on library usage, practices and organization (drawn from ILEA 1986a,b). Furthermore the emphasis began to move towards integrating work on gender into overall school policy, organization and disciplinary structures.

However there were still noticeable differences of orientation in much of the work mentioned above compared to those of the new discourses of management in the 1980s that were being produced in education and more widely. The emphasis within gender initia-tives until now had been on participation and personal experience rather than on management and rational planning. Moreover, because of the *ad hoc* and 'alternative' character of many of the earlier feminist initiatives (and the immense hostility with which they were confronted) change in this area was seen as highly political, relatively slow-moving and immensely unpredictable.

It was only in the late 1980s and early 1990s that feminist teachers began to perceive the need to fall in line with newly constituted orthodoxies about school management drawing on theories of schools as organizations and management systems (see for example, Handy and Aitken 1986). There were critics who viewed this management discourse as a new technology of power, a new 'moral technology' of management with a new set of male power relations. According to Ball, this management stance constitutes:

> a theoretical and practical technology of rationality geared to efficiency, practicality and control . . . It represents the bureaucratization of the structure of control . . . And it embodies a clear empiricist–rationalist epistemology. Organizational control and individual action are subsumed within a technical perspective.
>
> (Ball 1990c: 157)

Previous informal, often idiosyncratic models of school organization in which feminists had been able to insert themselves were now being replaced by new managerial regimes characterized by systems of 'line management' with clearly defined job descriptions and boundaries, spheres of competence, and more defined hierarchical management structures. This had several related implications. First, the new organizational practices cut across feminist-identified styles of working which tended to be more 'open, democratic, friendly, and collaborative, and less confrontational and competitive' (Marshall 1985; Powney and Weiner, 1991). Second, with its focus on such practices as target-setting, service-delivery, efficiency and 'quality', the kind of managers which such managerial cultures required were less likely to be women or men sympathetic to feminist issues.

Interestingly, as local education authorities began to develop overall policies on equal opportunities, feminists who had taken up local authority posts as inspectors and advisers to push through such policies (and who, as part of senior management frequently received 'training' in the management techniques described above) began to put pressure on feminist practitioners to 'manage' change more rationally and effectively, and in some senses, to treat gender initiatives like any other attempt at change, equivalent, say, to the adoption of a new reading scheme or alterations in staffing policy. Hazel Taylor, working in Brent, asserts the power of effective management as follows:

> The implementation of equal opportunities initiatives cannot be divorced from an appreciation of the effectiveness of school's management; a desire to change that is not supported by effective management techniques to bring change about is no more satisfactory than no intention of changing,

and can produce an extremely frustrating atmosphere for young teachers to work in.

(Taylor 1985: 131)

Feminists thus inserted themselves into this new managerial discourse by resorting to strategies around the 'management of change' and rational planning. For instance, in a handbook devoted to the 'principle, policy and practice' of equal opportunities, George cites identification of 'sources of support', strategies for change and coherence in approach, as central to the 'adoption and subsequent implementation of an effective equal opportunities programme' (George 1993: 1). The necessity for appropriate documentation is also highly prioritized, as is 'ownership' of policy.

The policy of producing a policy document can be one of the most effective ways of raising awareness of equality issues within the school/institution . . . The policy must clearly demonstrate ways in which it is designed to ensure that the talents and resources of all pupils/students can be utilised to the full . . . An involvement in the process will foster a climate of commitment and ownership which is essential to the success of the policy.

(George 1993: 9)

Additionally, criticisms were made of previous feminist initiatives for certain weaknesses of planning: for example, for failing to distinguish between long-term and short-term goals – say, between wider aims of changing pupil and teacher attitudes and the more simple tasks of de-sexing registers or developing non-sexist materials – or for being overly ambitious. To counter this, the *Genderwatch* pack (Myers 1986) provided information on how the broader aims of schools could be broken down into smaller, more manageable parts.

The pack is intended to help schools set realistic short, medium and long term goals and to monitor their success in achieving them. It is divided into three stages. Stage 1 has been devised to help set the scene, review what has happened so far and plan what needs to be done next. Stage 2 is issue specific . . . Stage 3 is subject specific, written to help teachers consider their subject area in relation to equality issues.

(Myers 1986: 1)

It was also important within the discourse of management of being 'seen' to make a difference. This was particularly crucial in such centrally funded vocational schemes as TVEI where failure to 'deliver' changes in, say, option choices or stereotyped career patterns, in the limited period offered by the schemes, was likely to put in jeopardy government support for the equal opportunities elements of the schemes. The necessarily slow progress of some of the earlier feminist initiatives, thus, seemed entirely incompatible with the deliberate fast pace and short-term nature of government funding requirements.

Networks and projects

During the 1980s, a decade of increasing government hostility in Britain towards those (particularly, local authorities) attempting to eradicate educational inequality as we have seen, feminist teachers (and other 'critical' educationists) were compelled to look elsewhere for forms of collaboration and support. They also were obliged to draw on their own resources to develop more autonomous approaches to change.

Some initiated projects of their own such as developing whole school policy on a range of equality issues. Such *teacher-initiated projects*, whether by individuals or groups of teachers, were likely to be small scale, and short-lived, with consequent problems of underfinancing and resourcing. Moreover, the majority of the teachers involved were usually at the lower end of the school hierarchy, and from the secondary rather than the primary sector. Yet these projects were nevertheless critical in providing a major challenge to conventional practitioner assumptions about gender, and in offering insights into how teachers could develop their own educational goals and implementation styles.

Teachers trying to promote change from the 'inside' faced a number of difficult questions. How could they impress others of the importance of gender as an educational issue, and convince the unconvinced? What was the best way to promote change within an educational institution? Could change be 'managed' and, if so, what role might senior management take? Given the 'political' nature of the work, how far could teachers go in challenging gender differences in school and more widely?

Millman (1987), for example, found the position of the teacher-activist in the hierarchy and within-school culture to be all important:

Established and respected teachers had considerably more influence on school policy than those on supply or in their probationary year . . . Moreover if the school already had a tradition of teacher-initiated debate on general curricular issues, the existing structures of staff and curriculum development was more likely to provide a forum within which research findings on gender could be presented to colleagues.

(Millman 1987: 260)

As we saw in Chapter 4, others became involved in *action research projects*, working collaboratively with educationists from different institutions. Researchers, usually from higher education, joined with teachers to intervene in the schooling process, for example, on pupil subject choice or to develop curriculum materials. By working cooperatively to challenge inequalities in education, the conventional distance between researchers and academics and teachers was also narrowed. The best known projects of this kind focused on the curriculum choices of girls, and in particular, their level of involvement in science and technology. The Girls and Technology Education project (GATE) investigated ways of improving the curriculum and assessment of craft, design and technology (CDT), and developing 'good practice'. The Girls into Science and Technology project (GIST) on the other hand, worked directly with teachers, attempting to reduce sex-stereotyping on the part of pupils and teachers, and promoting 'gender-fair' interaction in classrooms so that girls would feel encouraged to study scientific subjects.

Another approach, still within the action research framework, aimed at encouraging teachers to become independent researchers. May and Rudduck (1983) conducted a project in first and middle schools in Norfolk in which their goal was to raise awareness about sex-stereotyping in the early school years by encouraging teachers to explore the dynamics of their schools. This was to be achieved by enabling them 'to understand better their own practice as a basis for informing future curricular decisions'. Teachers volunteered to take part, and with the help of skilled researchers, designed and carried out investigations. May and Rudduck found the effects of such investigations difficult to assess. Would they have any long-term effect? Would the teachers continue with such research or put their skills to further use in the development of school policy? Could the data generated be useful for other schools?

Similar concerns also confronted the 'Schools Council Sex Differentiation Project' which, as we have seen, adopted the 'teacher–
researcher' approach and did much to legitimize both the area and
the method of producing innovation in schools (Millman 1987).
Based on the Schools Council's model of curriculum development
and innovation (see Chapter 3 for more detailed discussion of this
project), project teachers first developed small research studies of
their own, which replicated as far as possible social science methods of research and data collection. The findings from these small
scale studies were then fed back to the school as a stimulus to
discussion and eventual change. Sensitivity to 'audience' was a
feature of this form of teacher activity:

> Classroom research, particularly in the area of sex differen-
> tiation, is likely to raise some very sensitive questions and
> often teachers will find it hard to accept that their methods
> and interactions are sexist. In view of this, research findings
> will need to be presented in a full, thoughtful and objective
> manner so that teacher consciousness is raised as widely as
> possible.
>
> (Millman 1983: 31)

A later extension to this line of development within action research linked policies to eradicate educational inequalities more
clearly within discourses of management practice and practitioner
research. This form of action research locates the importance of
educational research in 'everyday practice' rather than as 'work
conducted by academics' (Guerney 1989: 14), utilizing the cycle of
reflection of the reflective practitioner in order to solve problems
of a practical nature in specific classroom or school contexts (see
Chapter 7 for a fuller discussion of this). Exploration of social
justice issues within this discourse was relatively weak despite an
underlying rhetoric of emancipation and empowerment as I have
written elsewhere (Weiner 1989a). However, more recently, equality
too has featured as an issue for this group of action researchers.
Neale (1991), for example, uses the 'practice-centred rationale' of
action research to investigate how he, as a senior teacher, could encourage implementation of equal opportunities in a boys' secondary
school, because:

> I believe my school has tended to exacerbate matters [prob-
> lems associated with equal opportunities issues] by reinforcing

sex, race and class stereotyping, and that we should try and liberate students from this oppression.

(Neale 1991: 26, 27)

The strategies developed to do this, for instance, establishing a school equal opportunities group, developing in-service training programmes, creating whole school policy, are not so different from feminist initiatives occurring a decade and a half earlier. What is remarkably different is the educational discourse utilized – of reflection, rational planning, personal development and liberal values of action research – rather than the passionate politically-challenging women-identified discourses of the earlier feminist initiatives. Inevitably, it seems, action researchers such as Neale indicate little awareness of the wide range of theoretical and practical debates informing initiatives on gender and education in previous years.

It is difficult to ascertain how influential any of these small-scale initiatives can ever be. Given the deep prejudices and sexist practices of teachers generally, to what extent can such relatively small and necessarily temporary initiatives be enduring? Kelly expresses her disappointment at the probable outcome of the GIST project thus:

We [the GIST team] never anticipated that a small project . . . could produce massive changes in traditional beliefs and practices. However we do confess to a sense of disappointment in the teachers' reactions, and to a scepticism about the extent to which the innovations which were developed during the life of the project will survive its absence.

(Kelly 1985: 138)

A more systematic approach to embedding concerns about gender inequality more firmly in mainstream educational structures was adopted by local authorities such as Brent and ILEA in London. In-service courses were designed around the concept of teacher–researcher with the aim of involving as wide a range of teachers as possible from the various sectors of education. Taylor working in Brent, rejected the top-down management approach to change as inappropriate and ineffective at the level of the classroom, preferring instead:

a bottom-up model [which] is harder to support and likely to produce divergence between institutions, but is the model philosophically most acceptable to the nature of the initiative... as it forces acknowledgement of the fact that much of the innovative work, both in defining the problems in providing an education for gender equality, and developing practice to bring it about, has been and is actually being done by teachers within their schools.

(Taylor 1985: 126)

Another strategy adopted by feminist educators was to develop *contact and communication networks* both for support and for knowledge dissemination – given that the development of action research and teacher initiated projects rely on access to information and advice on how to proceed. The existence of a network of teacher organizations has therefore been critical in encouraging innovation and reform. Such networks include: *teacher/subject groups*: such as Women in History, Women in Geography, Girls and Mathematics (GAMMA), Women in Computing, Women in Economics etc.; *women in education groups*: organized locally, in Hull, Oxford, Manchester, Cambridge, London etc.; *resource centres and newsletters*: for example, the Women's Educational Resource Centre and the London Women's Education Group with its journal *GEN*; *publishing ventures*: Pandora Press, the 'Gender and Education' series published by Open University Press, Virago etc.; and *learning materials collections*: for example, films, exhibitions, teaching and in-service packs on different subjects produced by such groups as GAMMA and in *Genderwatch*.

Feminist teachers also came together, as we have seen, in their *teacher unions*. Given the context of union work, they focused on different topics compared to the school-based initiatives, yet they faced similar obstacles – male dominated union hierarchies, low status, inability to influence the union agenda etc. For example, as early as 1978 a group of women in the National Union of Teachers (NUT) grouped together to respond to what they saw as the low priority given to women's rights issues in the union, the ghettoization of women in the lowest paid and poorest funded areas of education and the general domination of the union and its policy-making by men (reported in Women in the NUT 1981).

Prompted by this feminist assault and despite its flawed history concerning its women members (see Oram 1987), the NUT set the pace for union activity on gender issues in the 1980s by sponsoring a survey, 'Promotion for the Woman Teacher' (NUT 1981) with the Equal Opportunities Commission, drawing up 'model' job descriptions, providing advice on maternity benefits, and developing formal policy on gender for the profession generally. It also ran a series of training courses for women with the aim of promoting 'women's self-development, particularly in relation to their careers, their more active involvement in the Union and their role in establishing equal opportunities policies within their individual schools' (NUT 1986: 4).

Other education unions were less willing to take up what were considered by some as issues which divided their membership and which ran counter to prevailing (male) discourses on teachers' professional needs. However, most focused on women's issues in some form or other, establishing women's committees and/or regional panels (Association of University Teachers, AUT; National Association of Teachers in Further and Higher Education, NATFHE), developing guidelines on LEA equal opportunities policy (NATFHE) and publishing newsletters for their female members (AUT). Later, the proposed changes in schooling and in teachers' conditions of service heralded by the 1988 legislation stimulated a flurry of documentation on equal opportunities in the context of appointment, appraisal and promotion procedures (e.g. NUT 1990; NASUWT undated).

The new educational era

By the end of the 1980s, as we have seen, the British educational agenda had been transformed. A programme of legislation including the 1986 Education Act delegating more power to school governing bodies, the 1988 Education Reform Act (ERA) which included the introduction of a national curriculum and devolved (local) management to schools (LMS) and acts in 1992 and 1993 encouraging the privatization of public services, signalled the clear intention of the government to make a break with the past. Certainly the introduction of a national curriculum with the explicit aim of providing all children with the same curricular experiences seemed to address liberal feminist demands for common experiences within a core curriculum but as I suggest in Chapter 6, it was a particular cultural product that rendered women marginal to the main terrain of education. Also, the destruction of the Labour-controlled local authorities, many of which had been pioneers in terms of equality initiatives, and the cash restraints of rate and poll-capped authorities, meant that much of the earlier work on gender now became heavily circumscribed.

Some work nevertheless still continued: for example, teacher and action research, publications, networks and equal opportunities as part of professional development (WHEN 1991). Ironically, as funding and support for specific initiatives decreased, the rhetoric of equal opportunities became more pronounced in mainstream educational and government publications. And local authorities and higher education institutions rushed to call themselves equal opportunity employers!

Feminist practitioners reacted differently in different sectors of education. Reeling from massive amounts of work imposed on them by national curriculum requirements, practitioners at school level either suspended action for the meantime until a feminist regrouping could take place, or departed from education altogether for other more hospitable and compatible areas of activity. Those in higher education, such as myself, sought other ways to try to derive meaning and to sustain hope in the face of what we perceived as draconian and regressive government actions. Also, if working at the policy level was no longer available to us, we needed to create alternative 'spaces' in which to think about and review feminist impact on, and practice in, education. Why, we reflected, was policy on gender apparently going into reverse? Why was it happening now? Were there any grounds at all for optimism about the future? How could we understand past feminist activities in the context of present government priorities? Such questions led to increased feminist interest in the role of government in shaping gender relations in education not only in the UK but in other countries; first, to see if any patterns to gender policy were discernible and also to explore the micro-political implications of specific education policy discourses.

Educational policy and the construction of gender

Undoubtedly, for the reasons given above, there has been increased interest recently in the extent to which the power of the state is able to define and shape educational practices. However, feminists have long been aware of the relationship between state policy on education and the specific discourses on femininity and masculinity that emerge within schooling at different historical periods. In exploring government policy, Wolpe (1976) and Deem (1981), for example, provide insights into how masculinity and femininity has been constructed or produced within and through education in the post-1944 period; and thus how such constructions may be understood and challenged today. Arnot emphasizes the importance of such a field of study, and also that it is generally neglected by other (male-stream!) commentators on government policy. Furthermore she suggests that government education policy cannot be fully understood without such a gender dimension:

> it is my belief that the full significance of the last two decades of policy-making cannot be fully understood without more questions being asked about the gendered assumptions which underpin these educational reforms.
>
> (Arnot 1993: 187–8)

Moreover, Arnot suggests that accompanying what she calls a 'new sensitivity' (1993: 191) to the structures influencing gender dynamics, the state is now conceived as much more active in shaping gender politics, and sexual and gender oppression and regulation. Blackmore (1992) makes the point that state intervention in gender relations has always been a feature of education policy starting with the introduction of compulsory elementary education. Writing about the context of Australia in the 1870s, she argues that such an intervention shows the interrelationship of class, gender, pedagogy, practice and education policy-making.

> First, it was the first major intervention by the state in education and hence indicates a changing role of the state *vis-à-vis* the gender relations formed around family, education and work. Second, compulsory education changed the relationships between the working class and education, and between the middle and the working class. Third, it institutionalized through law the hegemony of a particular male style of education . . . Fourth . . . [it] produced a system which was able, within the same institutions, to offer gender-specific schooling based on a domestic educational ideology.
>
> (Blackmore 1992: 57)

We have already considered the impact of such nineteenth and early twentieth-century gendered forms of domestic ideology in Chapter 3. Moreover, these ideologies remained dominant in British education until well into the period of feminist practitioner activity mentioned earlier in this chapter. In her investigation of girls' education implicit in the ideologies of the Norwood, Crowther and Newsom Reports (Committee of the Secondary Schools Examinations Council 1943, Ministry of Education 1959 and Central Advisory Council for Education in England 1963 respectively), Wolpe concludes that whilst the three reports appeared to be grounded in reformist assumptions about the nature of an expanded system of mass education, they all 'provide an ideological basis for the perpetuation of an education system which does not open up new vistas or possibilities to the majority of girls' (Wolpe 1976: 157). Similarly, Deem (1981) characterizes the educational ideology of the post-World War II period as sustaining the belief of woman's primary place as in the home. From the radical Labour government of 1944–51, which was surprisingly resistant to extending such basic rights as equal pay to women (Dean 1991) through the high point of social democracy and the extension of the welfare state in the late 1960s to the breakdown of consensus about education and the decline of social democracy towards the end of the 1970s, there was little visible support for feminist goals or for any other than the broadest notions of sexual equality. In fact, even as the Sex Discrimination Act (Home Office 1975) was passed, the deepening economic crisis and related cut-backs in areas of the welfare state meant that its impact was relatively weak. As Deem (1981: 139) notes:

> The Great Debate of 1976/7 . . . did certainly consider the issue of women's education, and discuss the importance of preparing both boys and girls for roles in both the home and the labour market, but in the absence of positive follow-up to this in terms of actual educational policy change, the Debate remained a not very effective exercise in democratic participation.

So the years before Thatcherism and the education policies of the 1980s should not be perceived as a 'golden age' of educational equality but rather as a climate which allowed for individual feminist initiatives in education to take place provided they did not destabilize any existing educational priorities or agendas. It is my view that whilst the era of New Right policies from 1979 onwards fractured the social democratic project of the previous decades, its policy on gender was not noticeably different from other decades and in fact, some of its vocational initiatives gave a relatively higher profile to gender issues than ever before (Weiner 1989b).

However a number of factors served to highlight Thatcherite policy implications for gender. First, the attacks on local authorities and on municipal socialism which had used increased support for equality initiatives in the first half of the 1980s as part of their overt challenge to New Right policies, resulted in dramatic reversals in funding for equal opportunities work of any kind.

Second, notions of justice were reframed to address the perceived justice of the market and around individual choice and freedom, rather than related to notions of economic parity, collectivism, representation and democracy, as previously. In tackling what were perceived as the twin crises of capitalism and patriarchy (or authority), New Right discourses claimed a central position for the family.

According to Arnot, the family was to be a defence against socialism and state power, the basis of private property, the locus of consumption, the 'centre of affections', 'transmitter of traditions' and 'condition of authority' (Arnot 1992: 53). Given this multiplicity of responsibilities and also the centrality of the mother within such family discourses, the position of women within this ideological framework was not at all clear (particularly as it was a woman who was leading the New Right onslaught). This lack of clarity was especially visible within educational policy with its various aims of removing obstacles to individual progress, providing common experiences of schooling, producing a flexibly-skilled workforce to serve the needs of an ever shifting labour market, prioritizing certain kinds of knowledges (mathematics, science and technology) over others, elevating the patriarchal family as the main social and economic unit of capitalism and so on.

Its ideological impact on education is even less clear for feminists. These apparently contradictory pulls within education policy indicate neither coherence in New Right education policy nor a clear indication of what forms of femininity are most preferred. Is it the mother at home, the company 'wife', the part-time woman worker filling in the skills gaps where necessary, the dedicated professional or carer, the senior woman manager, the female industrial (or military?) physicist, or the individual, aspiring female middle-class politician?

In effect what this mix of conceptions of femininity has meant in practical terms is an implicit assumption within education policy that equality of opportunity is reasonably important for girls and boys, but that it should only be dealt with at the level of the individual. A 1992 HMI survey on classroom and curricular experience of girls is a useful example of this position. One of its findings is that 'it is the subtleties and nuances of provision that variation according to gender seems to make the most impact' (HMI 1992: 2). In the final report, the girls themselves, as the consumers, are allowed to set the priorities for what is needed (for the next stage in their careers) rather than the teachers or the HMI itself. Thus the girls identify qualifications, successful 'track record', reliability and 'becoming a balanced person' as most helpful for the future. Additionally,

the specific aspects of the curriculum which were identified as being important in preparation for working life included careers talks; 'challenge of industry' events; aspects of social studies; PSE-type courses; and, more generally, discussion in lessons and smaller groups. Girls also wanted to know how well they were doing and, in this connection, mentioned reports, continuous assessment and tests at appropriate times.

(HMI 1992: 14)

The point being made here is that concepts of equality and justice, for that matter, continue to exist within current government and New Right discourses, but in highly individualized and extremely weak forms. In Taylor's very useful overview of British government policy on equal opportunities policies post-1988, she implies that the lack of strong central policy and lack of commitment from the political administrations and educational status quo prior to the Thatcher era meant that equal opportunities was inevitably vulnerable. It occupied a fairly precarious place on policy agendas and therefore could be easily picked off when the time came.

The British experience shows the importance of strong policy frameworks and of the importance of making changes at an institutional level if equal opportunity initiatives are to be successful . . . such institutionalisation . . . needs to be achieved through planning and supported by the system. Most of the British initiatives lacked such support which would have ensured more long term change.

(Taylor 1991: 11)

Conclusions

In this chapter, I have attempted to provide an overview of the experiences gained in recent years from efforts made to challenge inequalities relating to gender in education and also to analyse the impact of government, and in particular the New Right, on gender policy-making and practice. It might seem that, currently, times are increasingly hard for feminist educators (teachers in particular) and there may seem to be few possibilities available for autonomous action. However, in seeking to put on record the past achievements of feminists and the strategies and tactics they developed to insert themselves in the discourses and to create counter-discourses, what I have tried to show is how feminism has also proved infinitely adaptable in finding niches to exploit and new audiences to galvanize into action.

It is also important to remember that the Conservative restructuring of education was to some degree a response to the gains that feminists and others had made in challenging conventional power relations and sexist practice within and outside education. The next two chapters suggest ways in which the feminist critique of, and challenge to, education can be sustained and developed to meet the inevitabilities of change demanded by future generations of feminist students, teachers and even politicians.

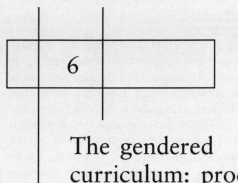

6

The gendered curriculum: producing the text

Until relatively recently, as we have seen, the changes and solutions put forward by feminist teachers and other educationists to challenge patriarchal relations in schooling and in education more generally (for example, for girls to do better at science or for school books to be non-sexist – see Chapter 5) have tended to be perceived as relatively unproblematic. The main struggle has been how best to get gender inequalities (alongside other social aspects of educational inequality) high(er) on the educational agenda. Concern about how to generate, implement and sustain change has been of less interest. However, after a decade or so of, admittedly patchy, feminist activity in education, the gains that have been made seem relatively modest. What has emerged is that where change has occurred it has tended to be restricted to relatively visible factors such as course content or staffing patterns; the success of initiatives has depended on the continuing and active commitment of individuals; and where 'activists' have left or 'burnt out', or when local policy priorities have changed, there has been an apparent reversion back to 'normal' sexist practices.

In order to understand the reasons for this, it is my view that we need to move beyond the easy answer or the rational solution and look much more closely at education to see how the 'normal-izing' and 'regulative' aspects of dominant discourses operate to subvert attempts at fundamental change. This chapter sets out to do this by exploring current understandings about the curriculum as gendered, and as a set of discursive practices in which girls and boys, teachers and pupils, different racial groups are differently and variously constituted as powerful or powerless, good or bad, feminine or masculine, workers or mothers etc. It will start with a discussion of the value of poststructuralist analysis in under-standing how gender relations are inscribed (or imprinted, etched) within curriculum practices and then consider three examples of how such an analysis can be helpful. Two of the studies concen-trate on specific subject areas, though in different sectors of edu-cation: Walkerdine (1988) explores pre-school and early school mathematics and Thomas (1990) investigates how subject areas, science and humanities in particular, are constructed in higher education. The third considers the relationship between policy and text in a study of British national curriculum documentation: in particular, the form of knowledge produced, how multiple closed texts have been used, the likely effect on present gendered meanings within schooling, and the utilization of curriculum by government for political and rhetorical reasons (Burton and Weiner 1990; Weiner 1993). The final section suggests an educational politics arising out of poststructural feminism which will also go some way to refuting the criticism that poststructural feminism is likely to be ineffective within feminist politics due to its inability to put forward a viable political programme (see Chapter 4).

The curriculum and poststructuralism

There has already been some discussion of feminist poststructural-ism and how it has been utilized with education contexts (see Chapter 4). I have suggested that its strength lies in its claim to creating new analytic frameworks for defining and exploring so-cial relations. I concentrate here, however, on how it may be helpful to our understanding of the emergence of specific curricu-lum formulations at specific historical and cultural periods (see Chapter 3 for an initial discussion of this). Briefly, poststructuralism relies on a number of central ideas. First, it views *language* as the common factor in any analysis of social organizations, power and individual consciousness. It is in language that our subjectivity as well as social organizations are defined, contested and constructed:

> The assumption that subjectivity is constructed implies that it is not innate, not genetically determined, but socially produced ... Language is not the expression of unique individuality: it constructs the individual's subjectivity in ways which are socially specific.
>
> (Weedon 1987: 21)

Further, poststructuralism assumes that meaning is constructed within language and is not guaranteed by what the author intends. Thus, for example, any analysis of the impact of curriculum policy necessarily has to consider its interpretation as well as its intention or impact.

Second, poststructuralism takes *universals* and *truths* to be problematic and open to scrutiny, arising out of specific historical changes. It seeks to analyse in what ways those ideas have become *universal* or *normalizing* – hence, as Ball argues (1990b: 2), 'the idea of a judgement [is] based on what is normal and thus what is abnormal'.

Third, it uses the principle of *discourse* to show how power relationships and subjectivity are constituted. Discourses are structuring mechanisms for social institutions, modes of thought and individual subjectivities. They are:

> practices that systematically form the objects of which they speak ... Discourses are not about objects; they do not identify objects, they constitute them and in the process of doing so conceal their own invention.
>
> (Foucault 1974: 49)

We need therefore to scrutinise specific discursive curriculum practices to ascertain why, at a particular time, one particular statement or curriculum formulation appeared rather than another.

Fourth, drawing on Foucault, *power–knowledge* is used as a single configuration of ideas and practice that constitute a discourse. Thus the knowledge that is produced as truth is the knowledge that is linked to the system of power which produces and sustains it. Even if, then, the 'political' nature of curriculum may seem a-political – 'nothing could seem more a-political, more cognitive, perhaps more boring, than analysing children's learning of maths' (Walkerdine 1988: 211) – this is far from the case. In fact, as we have seen in the bitterly contested disputes about school history and English in the British national curriculum (e.g. Kettle 1990; Clanchy 1993), the curriculum is central to the production and maintenance of any political and social regime. Curriculum is also heavily implicated in the production of regulative understandings: it is as much concerned about what it means to be an intelligent pupil, a loyal worker or the good mother as about the legitimization of certain forms of knowledge.

Fifth, poststructuralism therefore mounts a *challenge to the liberal humanist* commitment to the individual, its claims to 'knowing rationality', and 'in which *man* is the originator of his thoughts and speech' (Weedon 1987: 173). Curriculum is thus enmeshed in the normalizing tendencies of the existing social order.

> It is my contention that the modern order is founded upon a rational, scientific, and calculating form of government, a government which claims to describe and control nature, according to natural laws. Thus mathematics can be understood as absolutely central to the production of this order.
>
> (Walkerdine 1988: 211)

If, then, reason is value-laden and the truth, socially produced, discursive authority (who controls the agenda) is of paramount importance. Bodies of knowledge emerge at specific historical moments to account for the 'real' or the 'natural'. Why, we should ask, have mathematics, science, technology and history been so highly prioritized in recent British curriculum formulations? An example suggested by Walkerdine of a specific body of knowledge with normalizing features is 'child development', a core element of all initial teacher education courses for much of the twentieth century. Here, identification of the 'normal pupil', the 'well-socialized girl or boy' or the 'normal sequence of learning' imply a set of social practices which necessarily also provides room for a pathology for those whose behaviour defies such practices. Thus, these practices, outside which no child (or teacher) can stand, provide systems of classification, regulation and normalization whereby the 'position' of each child is read:

> I . . . use the concept of *positioning* to examine further what happens when such readings are produced and how children become *normal* and *pathological*, fast and slow, rote-learning and displaying real understanding and so on.
>
> (Walkerdine 1988: 204)

Accordingly, what we consider appropriate behaviour for children might appear commonsensical and 'normal' but, in fact, is manufactured and infused with power connotations. Drawing on Foucault, the concept of *power* used here does not rely on physical threat or overt ambition to dominate, rather it produces the willing subject: 'power ... is productive of social identity rather than instances of repression, violence or coercion' (Popkewitz 1988b: 31).

In fact, Popkewitz notes that when educational psychology emerged in the United States in the first two decades of the twentieth century, it was utilized to help expand the process of rationalization into new areas of personal conduct. Thus, the corporate drive for efficiency and rationalization of work processes was extended to schooling by means of a new language or discourse. The language of psychology, according to Popkewitz: 'created a way to reason about social conduct as defined in tasks to be evaluated in relation to universal attributions of individuals and notions of efficiency' (Popkewitz 1988b: 16). In this case, psychology certainly was not neutral, neither was it an acknowledged means of selecting school knowledge. Rather, by creating the 'psychologization of social phenomena' which was articulated as 'true', the way school subjects were taught reflected dominant values of 'those who have the power to give definition to reality' (Popkewitz 1988b: 16). As we can see, pedagogical approaches are inscribed within such normative practices. Thus in Walkerdine's deconstruction of pedagogy (see Chapter 4) she shows how the ideology of progressive pedagogy which is conceived of in terms of the liberation of children, is simultaneously oppositional to the liberation of their female teachers.

As we also saw in Chapter 4, poststructuralism has two main aims. It seeks to *deconstruct*, to analyse the operations of difference and the way in which meanings are made to work. It also offers the possibility for the production of a *counter-discourse* (or reverse discourse) which challenges meaning and power. Feminist poststructuralism likewise offers possibilities for the production of analytic frameworks and counter-discourses though with a prevailing main aim of privileging feminist interests in understanding and transforming existing patriarchal relations. As Jones points out, feminist poststructuralism is characterized by '"positive" uncertainty through a focus on complexity and diversity in thinking about gender' (Jones 1993: 158). Thus in the context of education, feminist poststructuralism moves beyond the female-as-deficient or female-as-victim models by:

> provide[ing] new possibilities for understanding girls' socialisation or the 'production of girls', which go beyond seeing girls primarily as 'disadvantaged' and socialised within oppressive patriarchal structures.
>
> (Jones 1993: 157)

Having considered how poststructuralist and feminist analyses can be applied more generally to curriculum and pedagogic practices, I now turn to specific studies to show how such analyses are possible in a range of curriculum contexts.

School mathematics

Walkerdine identifies two reasons for her examination of children's reasoning in pre-school and early school mathematics. First, in questioning liberal humanism's aim of eventual mastery over the physical world, she chose mathematics because for many it is synonymous with rational thought and enquiry:

> For Piaget, and for many in early education mathematics *is* reasoning. Logico-mathematical structures are the structures of rational thought. To develop 'mathematical concepts' in children carries the supreme task of creating reasoners and all that entails.
>
> (Walkerdine 1988: 6)

Her investigation thus proposed to 'prise apart', to deconstruct, psychological and pedagogic claims or truths about children's learning, and to provide alternative interpretations or 'readings'. Walkerdine further argues that early mathematical education depends heavily on being inscribed in the wider body of discursive practices which may be described as 'child-centred'. As we have seen, Walkerdine's main criticism of progressive pedagogies centres on their adoption as marking a shift from overt to covert forms of regulation. Thus, regulatory practices are concealed beneath an apparent intentionality of child-centredness to extend 'freedom' and 'creativity'; hence this examination of how the regulative features of child-centredness are established within mathematics education.

For the purposes of this chapter, I concentrate on two aspects of Walkerdine's work: her exploration of semantic practices of children within mathematics education, and her various studies of gender and school mathematics (1988, 1989). The empirical data for the early years study comes from two sources; the first is a set of mother–daughter conversations, each lasting approximately two hours, of 15 middle-class and 15 working-class girls with an average age of 3.9 collected by Barbara Tizard, and the second is Walkerdine's data on the conversations of six pre-school children, three girls and three boys, aged between 2.5 and 3.5.

In the study, Walkerdine argues that relational terms such as 'same' and 'different', 'more' or 'less', perceived as central to children's acquisition of a mathematical vocabulary, take on meaning within particular sets of cultural practices. According to Walkerdine, 'context' is not simply a given but is actively constructed and created. Thus, mathematical words and concepts which are held to signify cognitive development are also used in the practices of everyday life. They are not only generated within the classroom, but are socially produced: 'these relational dynamics . . . are produced in relation to aspects of social practices which are culturally and historically specific' (Walkerdine 1988: 12).

The meanings that children will make of certain words will therefore be shifting and elusive, reliant on various social factors within and beyond the perimeter of the school. Thus the utilization of mathematical language by children is highly complex, organized around the power relations of the moment: 'on the basis of the particular relationship between participants: who is in a position, allowed, and permitted to say what to whom and with what effects' (Walkerdine 1988: 12). Of particular importance is the social nature of such language as is exemplified in Walkerdine's account of how children work with size and quantity relations. Here, she looks at how such terms as 'short' and 'tall' and 'more' or 'less' find expression:

> We have seen that height is referred to in a variety of ways and that *tall* is only used in specific circumstances. In each case the height being referred to is that of the child or other children. Because, for children, the salient characteristic is that they grow *taller*, it is unlikely that they would be referred to as *short*, it would be likely to be *not tall enough* or some such phrase. It is equally possible, of course, that in

other contexts with other topics *short* may be appropriate
and would be used.

(Walkerdine 1988: 18)

'More' is a term of particular interest to Walkerdine. She points
out that while 'more' as a term is used both in the classroom and
the home, the implicit meanings will differ for different class groups.
In the middle-class home, 'more' may be used positively as a
question – 'Do you want more drink?' In working-class contexts,
'more' is likely be negatively framed as an impossible demand –
'You can't have more' (Jones 1993: 163). Thus, the class position
of the families involved in the studies (as it, say, relates to the
amount of money available to the family) may be viewed as a
crucially important feature in children's mathematical vocabulary.

The bourgeois child's conception of quantity is similar to
that of the school. The task for the working class child is to
move from one set of meanings to another – a difficult tran-
sition when the terms used are the same, but the meanings
are implicitly different, and not made explicitly available.

(Jones 1993: 163)

Further, the terms used in the mother–daughter conversations (as
with teacher–pupil conversations) Walkerdine suggests, should not
be viewed as merely a matter of turn-taking. The positioning of
the mothers and daughters within specific conversational practices
denotes a dynamic relating to unequal power relationships.

Centrally implicated, therefore, is an analysis of power: there
are not two equal participants. Furthermore, the meanings
created within such practices relate to the power and relationships inscribed within them.

(Walkerdine 1988: 31)

Walkerdine's study points to the inadequacy of previous linguistic systems within 'the perceptual universalities and object world'
of cognitive psychology in which maturity and complexity are
gained through 'a step-wise progression of features' (1988: 29).
Instead, she shows a world of the child which is not fixed and
static but 'slippery and mobile' (1988: 30). Specifically the analysis
allows for complexity, enabling links to be made between mathematical terms, the purpose for which they are used, and the
precise context of their use; and for recourse to social rather than
cognitive explanations for children's linguistic performance.

Walkerdine, here and in other studies (e.g. Walden and Walkerdine 1982) also highlights the implication of gender relations in the power–knowledge of mathematical education discourses. She notes that in relation to judgements made of girls' performance of mathematics, 'proofs' are produced which attest to their inadequacies in relation to boys. The point she seeks to make here is of the importance of seeing how girls are positioned within these discourses:

> I am not setting out to demonstrate the *real* . . . proof that girls *really* can do maths or boys actually do not have real understanding. Rather it is how these categories are produced as signs that I am interested in and how they 'catch up' the subjects, position them, and in positioning create a truth. For is not girls' bid for 'understanding' the greatest threat of all to a universal power or a truth that is invested in a fantasy of control of 'woman'?
>
> (Walkerdine 1988: 208)

If activity, then, is regarded as evidence of understanding, then the 'good' behaviour of the girls – hard-working, neat and helpful – is produced as evidence of lack of (or lesser quality of) understanding. Thus, according to Walkerdine, evidence of 'real understanding' of mathematics depends on a set of practices involving: how accomplishments are read as signifying 'real understanding'; explanations dependent on the other characteristics defining the learner; and a 'complex investment in desire . . . in proving the presence or absence of certain qualities' (1988: 208). Despite girls' relatively good performance in mathematics in the early years, every effort is seemingly made to diminish this achievement, for example, by attributing girls' success to the mediocre characteristics of rule-following and rote-learning. Further, in the secondary school, boys are frequently entered for examinations despite poor results in their preliminary assessments or 'mocks', and girls excluded, despite good performance (Walden and Walkerdine 1982. See similar patterns for black pupils in Wright 1987).

The point being made here is that whatever 'reality' might be, to focus on the way 'reality' is interpreted or 'read' is more helpful to our understanding of the social practices that govern educational discourses than are any attempts to 'prove' the existence or non-existence of certain personal qualities or abilities conducive to learning.

Gender and science

The study which forms the basis for this section (reported in Thomas 1990) set out to examine the experiences of male and female undergraduates in British higher education, and the meanings those students attach to their experiences. The main aim of the study was to consider the relationship between the 'culture' of certain subjects and the 'common-sense constructions of masculinity and femininity' (Thomas 1990: 8). A more specific objective was to identify why so few women take physical science subjects in higher education. The study took the form of semi-structured, tape-recorded interviews with 96 students (half male and half female) and 12 members of staff in three universities. It concentrated on two dualisms in particular, those of masculinity/femininity and science/arts. Thus the research included both women and men in order to look for difference and similarity within higher education curriculum areas, choosing physics and English as the main subject areas. Physics was selected because it is both studied by relatively few women and is seen as 'the most objective, rigorous and, indeed, successful of pure sciences' (Thomas 1990: 8) and English because of its largely female student intake and its central position in the liberal disciplines.

Though the study has some features of poststructural feminism such as an interest in how meanings are made and how male–female dualisms may be deconstructed, it does not overtly draw on poststructuralist ideas. However, it explores gender relations in the context of specific curriculum discourses and practices, thus lending itself to poststructuralist analysis. For the purposes of the discussion, I focus here on the way science is experienced by students, particularly by female students.

In considering how students construct science as a subject of study, Thomas found that the decision to study science is made not only in relation to other subjects but arises also from schooling and family influences: 'Obviously personal inclination is very important, but personal inclination can often arise from having been taught by an exceptional teacher, or having a scientist parent who helps with homework' (Thomas 1990: 43). Students appear to 'insert' themselves into the science discourse by presenting themselves as people having particular qualities for their chosen subject. The incompatibility of the arts and sciences is a major theme as is female students' concern to be 'as good as a man'

(1990: 44). Moreover, the science students appear to make sense of their discipline through a series of dualisms in which the values embodied in science are perceived as *lacking* in the humanities. The discourse of science is of dominance and superiority typified in the use of dualisms as follows:

Physics	*'Other'*
fundamental	tangential
certain	uncertain
progressive	static
infinite	finite
difficult	easy
hard	soft
understanding	rote learning
relevant	irrelevant
useful	useless

(Thomas 1990: 47)

Such dualisms are extremely powerful in liberal humanist discursive frameworks, as we have seen, so it should not be at all surprising that they are forcefully articulated by those being initiated into what is regarded as a high status body of knowledge. Students' statements about the nature of physics serve to reveal its discursive power as universalistic and fixed:

'it's fundamental in the way the world works';

'the implication of it affects the whole world, it's everything, everything you do, and demonstrates how things work and why things work';

'it's an open-ended subject . . . [other subjects] come to an end . . . But with physics, it can go on for ever, virtually';

'I think it's more a way of thinking than knowledge really . . . a way of tackling problems'.

(quotations from students, Thomas 1990: 47–9, 51)

All but one of these statements came from male students.

Linked with students' perceptions of the epistemological frameworks utilized with the discourse of science are their realities of actual study of the subject. The science departments are characterized by a *formality* of pedagogy which involves definitive *authority* of tutors and the *passivity* and dependence of the students, the overwhelming use of standard 'lecture', the *abstract* nature of subject content which seems to some students irrelevant to the outside world, and the heavy amount of *prescribed* and *controlled* laboratory work.

> The formality of staff–student relationships was reflected in the conventionality of the teaching methods used. The science students had very full timetables; these consisted mainly of lectures with some lab sessions and problem classes or tutorials (the latter being much less frequent on the physical science course).
>
> (Thomas 1990: 55)

What may be surprising is that so high status an academic discipline relies so heavily on *rote-learning*. Thomas reports that for most students, physics is not a subject which demands any 'real' understanding, unlike pre-school and early school maths: 'It's just proved my ability to learn chunks of knowledge, chunks of pages and books, and reproducing them the day after, then forgetting it, then you have to learn it again for next year's exams' (1990: 57).

Yet, if a body of knowledge is perceived as unique, fixed and contained with the hierarchies implicit in strong boundary maintenance and framing (Bernstein 1971), the importance for students (particularly at undergraduate level) to absorb and digest its main principles has some meaning. In contrast to the progressive pedagogies criticized by Walkerdine above, here dominant social practices are openly and forcefully underlined. All the students seem very aware of what is expected of them and what the 'rules of the game' are. Yet like progressive pedagogies, the discursive practices of these pedagogies are regarded as 'normal' and 'commonsense', even though, as we shall see later, some female students have difficulties in staying within the boundaries presented.

Thus students suffer who do not have the 'right' characteristics for the physics culture. One such student, Jane, reported liking the subject but hating the course, contrasting it unfavourably with her experience of physics at school which presented maths and science as 'nice, chatty, qualitative subjects' (Thomas 1990: 63). She presented herself as 'artistic', regretting the need for the specialization demanded in the course. Another such student, Mark, positioned himself within the science discourse as rejecting the values of the physics department and of academic life generally: 'that is he rejects the pervasive competitiveness and individualism . . . making comments like "I'm just not an academic basically"' (Thomas 1990: 64).

Of the students in the study, the women, who formed about a quarter of the overall student population in the sciences, were positioned very differently from the men. They tended not to see themselves as 'applied physicists' or as 'theoreticians' or even as 'physicists' as most men did, because of the perceived seriousness, status and weightiness of such professional designations. According to one female student, 'physics people have a reputation for being really boring and square and working all the time with computers and things' (Thomas 1990: 131).

In fact, Thomas suggests that the female science students did not see themselves as individuals at all but as a homogenous group, conscious of being different. They expressed feelings of being singled out, self-conscious, unusual, visible. For instance, tutors appeared to learn the women's names before those of the men. Yet none of the female students seemed able to 'look underneath' or deconstruct what was happening to them; none described themselves as victims of discrimination even if they registered surprise and awkwardness at their visibility in 'a masculine preserve' (Thomas 1990: 123). Significantly, science tutors appeared equally unable to deal adequately with their female students and more puzzled than anything else about how to treat them. Thus, women were perceived as an oddity and treated carefully for fear of them doing something untoward.

In order to cope with this positioning as the Other, most female students actively worked to reposition themselves within the discourse, to try and take up positions both as successful scientists *and* as women. The problem they faced was that the science education discourse denied this configuration. For example, Debbie dealt with the contradiction of being both a woman and a scientist by becoming more 'feminine'; 'in this way', Thomas (1990: 123) suggests, 'men's idea of what constitutes "femininity" is strengthened, rather than weakened, by their interactions with the female science students'. Women are thus revealed as actively constituting a discourse that relegates them to a position of marginality. Marianne, in contrast, took the subject position that identified her as 'as good as a man'. Making the contrast with her feelings of stupidity at sixth form college – 'I really felt a "stupid woman", you know, every time you said something or did something wrong in the lab, there was a comment' – she presented herself as happier at university: 'But the lads here are great. They treat you just the same' (Thomas 1990: 125). The power of male students to construct and define Marianne as a student remained unchallenged.

Another subject position for female science students within this discourse was to be a 'serious scientist'. Lesley opted for this: 'tries to get herself accepted not as a woman, but as a serious scientist, which, for her, meant taking on masculine traits and values' (Thomas 1990: 125). In reflecting on what constitutes appropriate or inappropriate dress for women scientists, Lesley viewed femininity as something which can be discarded, removed, altered according to the needs of the occasion:

> For Lesley, then, to be taken seriously as a scientist means leaving behind girlish things and taking on masculine values and attributes . . . Women cannot be equal with men unless they, figuratively speaking, become men themselves.
>
> (Thomas 1990: 126)

This subject position rejects feminism in favour of individual superiority: 'she [Lesley] is as much in competition with other women as she is with men' (1990: 126). What becomes clear, however, is that for female students such as Lesley, 'femininity' is inscribed within the power–knowledge of the science education discourse but is also available to be utilized, shaped and acted on.

In this relatively brief 'dip' into one part of Thomas's study of gender and subject, I have attempted to provide an alternative reading rather than undermine the author's intention or analysis. In so doing, I identified from the study the set of regulative practices within which students and lecturers are positioned, and also gave attention to the active participation of subordinate groups in the production of discursive practices. Not surprisingly given the strength and power of curriculum practices in the science subjects, there is little indication of the presence of a feminist counter-discourse (except, perhaps, in the support networks established by a few of the female students to counter the individual ethos of the department). This provides a contrast to the student experience of humanities courses also reported in the study, where feminism has a presence both in course content and in student's understanding of their own positions within humanities curriculum practices.

Reading curriculum texts

The main aim of this section is to draw attention to another form of curriculum study – the analysis of curriculum and policy texts. In particular, I reflect on a recent programme of research, with which I was involved, focusing on British national curriculum documentation (Burton and Weiner 1990; Weiner 1992a, 1993). (I will refer to this as the national curriculum study.) Briefly, the study focused on a range of curriculum documentation (on testing and assessment, viz. 'TGAT', and on the subject areas of English, mathematics, science, history and on cross-curricular themes), identifying in particular 'race' and gender issues. Through a close scrutiny of curriculum texts, the aim was to identify the overt and covert policy intentions of government in the hope that new meanings might emerge, less visible in the heat of policy introduction and implementation.

The study was informed to some extent by poststructuralist understandings, particularly on the centrality of texts in new curriculum formulations. The main aims, however, were to unpack or deconstruct curriculum policy on issues of equality and difference, and to create and insert a feminist counter-discourse into the curriculum debate. The categories of analysis used to shape the study were thus consciously chosen to reflect these aims: location of equality issues within the texts, differences in positioning of students, and epistemological foundations and implications. Ultimately we were concerned with political action as an early paper from the study indicates: 'our main purpose is to clarify possibilities for future action by attempting to understand the implications of current policy-making' (Burton and Weiner 1990: 205).

The study of texts

Text and how it should be read is a central feature of poststructuralism, as we have seen. Arising from this, interest in how texts, especially school textbooks, are used within education has been comparatively recent (e.g. Apple 1986; Castell *et al.* 1989; Apple and Christian Smith 1991; Christian Smith 1993). The main aim of such attention has been to view texts as heavily inscribed in educational practices and emanating from a complex interplay of political, economic and cultural forces – rather than merely delivering 'the facts'. Apple and Christian Smith (1991) point out that school texts are conceived by people with interests, and published within the political and economic constraints of markets, resources and power. They present particular perspectives of reality, and of selecting and organizing knowledge and so contribute to our common-sense understandings of the 'reality' of culture and knowledge. Moreover, specific forms of text production are often the outcome of extensive battles and compromises.

> The [text], it is not melodramatic to declare, really is the battleground for an intellectual civil war, and the battle for cultural authority is a wayward, intermittently fierce, always protracted and fervent one.
>   (Inglis, quoted in Apple and Christian Smith 1991: 4)

It is easier to deconstruct the specifics of current British curriculum practices and texts if we also understand them as outcomes of the protracted battles between government and teachers in the mid-1980s. Despite the overlay of rational planning and user-friendly language, the apparent seamlessness of the national curriculum texts and the positioning of teachers as receivers of fixed and prescriptive pedagogic practices serve to reveal the unequal power relations of the enterprise.

In fact, struggles over who should control school texts have tended to emerge at times of political change: in the United States, as a part of the extensive movement to enhance the democratic rights of teachers, and in Britain, more recently, with the advent of more heavily prescribed syllabuses accompanying the national curriculum. Accompanying such changes, texts can be both retrogressive and progressive according to Apple and Christian Smith (1991), either enforcing systems of moral regulation or assisting teachers in their work within the democratic process. Feminists have added to the debate by arguing that popular, as well as school, texts play a central role in the production of patriarchal relations and in the construction of femininity (e.g. Taylor 1993).

If the perspectives on textual practices seem complex, textual analysis, that is how to 'read' and research texts, appears equally labyrinthine. The conventional goal of the educational critic is the identification of bias or distortion in the curriculum or policymaking and this has also been a principal aim of text research (as illustrated in the national curriculum study). Research method, however, has been problematic. In the past, according to Gilbert

(1989), the most popular approach to text analysis in the social sciences utilized 'scientific' and 'quantitative' analytical frameworks:

> Aiming for an objective, systematic and statistically reliable method, researchers developed techniques for the quantitative description of text meaning content. Often these were simple frequency counts of the occurrence of pre-specified words, phrases or other semantic units.
>
> (Gilbert 1989: 62)

However, in placing heavy emphasis on the frequency of the chosen semantic unit and divorced from any textual meaning, quantitative textual analysis has been dismissed as reductionist and superficial. Recognizing such 'objective' approaches to text analysis as demonstrably partial, Anyon (1979) called for a link to be made between the texts and conflicting and competing social practices and interests. In subordinating method to description and explanation, she also legitimized possibilities for basing analysis of texts on interpretation and deconstruction.

More recently, frameworks for text analysis have come to be seen neither as permanent descriptions of social relations or models created from stable categories. Research processes have grown more flexible and interactive, operating 'as dynamic responses to problems in particular situations, subject to test and alteration in experience' (Gilbert 1989: 65). However, any explicit 'method' of poststructuralist textual analysis is difficult to identify. Rather, Gilbert claims that work containing elements of the following might be conceived of as poststructuralist:

> critique rather as a continuous rewriting of ideology in contesting discourses . . . includ[ing] a permanent auto-critique in our analysis . . . see[ing] interpretation and critique as an historically grounded social practice . . . recogniz[ing] discursive practices . . . [as] frameworks for exerting power.
>
> (Gilbert 1989: 62)

How do these discussions, largely about school texts, help with the study of policy documentation? Policy texts clearly constitute a form of discourse; that is, they embody both a language and requisite social practices. Policy documents (like school texts) also can be understood as signifying discursive practices, messages from which need to be read as ideological and political artifacts, produced at specific historical and political contexts. Certainly, such an analysis of national curriculum documentation reveals an entirely new discursive framework through which government has sought to extend its power over teachers. This is characterized by a continuous stream of glossy, persuasive 'teacher-proof' curriculum texts which teachers are obliged to read, absorb and practise. The emphasis is on conformity: 'Teachers and schools will not be free to pick and choose, or to decide to modify the requirements for some pupils . . . They can always do *more* than is required . . . but they must not do less' (DES 1989b).

The character of the new social relations of the curriculum is further emphasized by the production of a new language. Numerous new terms have been produced (e.g. 'Programmes of Study', 'Key Stages') each of which is 'feather-bedded' in user-friendly explanations of the precise specificity of its meaning. The new language implies a technocratic rationality that serves to downgrade practitioner concerns. Parallels may be drawn between these developments in Britain and Apple's account of curriculum changes in the United States.

> The language of efficiency, production, standards, cost-effectiveness, job skills, work discipline, and so on – all defined by powerful groups and always threatening to become the dominant way we think about schooling – has begun to push aside concerns for a democratic curriculum, teacher autonomy, and class, gender, and race equality.
>
> (Apple 1986: 154)

Significantly, implementation of the national curriculum in its present form was possible *only* through the speedy production and distribution of the texts and through teachers' receipt and 'reading' of the texts. Moreover, the pressure on teachers to 'deliver' the new curriculum and the manner in which the texts were created and presented (by bureaucrats rather than practitioners) were unique to the British education system. Such textual practices ensured that teachers and schools were positioned to respond rapidly to change rather than await initiation through in-service training. However, the sheer volume of documentation also meant that few were able to keep up with all the required changes – and the resultant disquiet led to a regrouping and repoliticization of an otherwise subdued profession.

Equality and difference in curriculum texts

In terms of the national curriculum study's explicit aims, the first was to focus on the extent to which equality issues *appeared* in the documentation. We found that whilst there seemed to be a general rhetorical commitment to equal opportunities emanating from the texts, little attention had been paid to the existing body of research depicting the endemic nature of racism, sexism and other forms of discrimination. In fact, much of the documentation was either totally dismissive of, or apathetic to, equality issues. For example, the final mathematics working party report was scathing about multicultural and antiracist strategies that had been developed in mathematics education: 'we believe that this attitude [the multicultural approach] is misconceived and patronising'. Instead, priority was to be given to the generic knowledge, skills and competencies which children would need 'for adult life and employment in Britain in the twenty-first century' (National Curriculum Mathematics Working Group 1988: 87). Further, little help was evident generally for the development of pedagogical approaches to counter discrimination. Significantly, government hostility to equality issues was revealed by its failure to produce (as promised) specific cross-curricular advice on equality issues. Thus, *absence* from the documentation, i.e. what is left out, is as important as what is kept in.

Another focus for the study was on any differences in the *positioning* of pupils and students within the new curriculum formulations. Clearly pupils were not positioned equally, despite the textual overlay of rhetoric on equality (namely the promise of pupil entitlement, equality of access). Thus, on the one hand, the legislation ruled that there was a *common* set of subjects to be taught to all pupils; yet contradictorily many students were placed in subordinate positions to others or even excluded altogether as in the case of children with disabilities for whom 'disapplication' could be sought. Girls, once again, were implicitly produced as 'different' from the male-as-norm mainstream when choice was reintroduced for students at 14 plus. On the basis of previous experience, it was inevitable that when presented with subject choice, girls would be likely to 'choose' to do the single rather than double science option or to drop 'male' subjects if allowed. Thus, our conclusions were that earlier conventionally stereotyped patterns were likely to be re-established as greater choice of optional subjects increased at 14 plus (Key Stage 3). Significantly, pupils taught in the private (or public school) sector were inscribed as a different sort of 'other' in their exclusion from the requirements of the national curriculum. The implications of this seemed clear: an increased regulation of proletariat schooling was set alongside the wish of government that élite education should remain unchallenged and unshackled. In sharp contrast, inner-city pupils (although overtly included in the new curriculum practices) were also differently positioned as unlikely to be able to study on an equal footing with other pupils because of inadequate resourcing of the wider curriculum by the poorer urban local authorities.

The *epistemological* basis of the curriculum texts was another point of exploration for the study. Not unexpectedly, the study revealed a monocultural and retrogressive bias in the new curriculum formations. Thus, despite some minimal reference to the multiracial nature of British society, a perspective of western Christianity was advanced which served to render all other religious groupings as marginal. For example, it was stated that any new syllabus for Religious Education 'must reflect the fact that the religious traditions in this country are mainly Christian' (DES 1989a). The potential for creating religious conflict resulting from this normalizing of Christianity and for pathologizing 'minority' community religions did not go unnoticed (Troyna and Carrington 1990).

The specific epistemological foundations of the national curriculum were further revealed in attempts to forge a new (or rather, nineteenth-century) reading of what it means to be British. Pressure from government to increase the amount of *British* history in the school curriculum, for example, gave teachers little choice but to emphasize Britain's 'glorious' past. Hence the expectation was that 'programmes of study should have at the core the history of Britain, the record of its past and, in particular, its political, constitutional and cultural heritage' (National Curriculum History Working Group 1990: 189).

The newly created world of the national curriculum was also to be virtually 'woman-free'. Women's issues were accorded low priority across all the subject areas, such that few topics were entirely devoted to women. For instance, in the early history documentation, of the named individuals, white European males far outweighed any other representative group, as Gill (1990) points out, such that national curriculum history was still to be the history of 'great' white men.

Moreover there was an implicit assumption within national curriculum texts that knowledge is discrete – boxed under subject headings (English, mathematics etc.) – with minimal attention given to (non-mandatory) cross-curricular possibilities. This atomization was also evident inside curricular areas, such as mathematics and science, so that within-discipline knowledge also suffered from over-fragmentation and over-differentiation. Further, implications of the universality of science and maths curricula in particular, like the science department in Thomas's study, revealed conservative assumptions about the nature of knowledge and its pursuit which:

> assumes an anachronistic image of the inquirer as a socially isolated genius who selects problems to pursue, formulates hypotheses, devises methods to test hypotheses, gathers observations, and interprets the results of the enquiry . . . the reality is that most science research today is quite different.
> (Harding 1986: 248)

How does a study such as this assist our understanding of curriculum policies and practices? One important point is that curriculum texts need to be analysed as constructions of experiences and knowledges rather than 'neutral' transmitters of common-sense professional ideas and practices. They need also to be read as a fluid relationship between author's (government's) intention and readers' (teachers') interpretation. How we interpret the knowledges and prescriptions of the British national curriculum depends on where we are positioned in the education system. A primary teacher, a headteacher or a school governor is each likely to have different responses to texts confronting them. The interpretation of texts thus depends on the multiplicity of subjectivities that accompany their readers – as can be seen by the heated discussion which resulted from the publication of the history curriculum document (Weiner 1993). And the particular analysis offered here is the consequence of specific biographical, ideological and professional concerns.

What, then, are the possibilities of pursuing feminist goals within education given the bleak discursive practices reported in the studies as outlined above? It seems to me that there is some room for manoeuvre. As Ball remarks in the last paragraph of his book on British education policy 'the making of national policy still begs questions about the implementation and realisation of reform in schools and classrooms. The struggles over interpretation and accommodation go on' (Ball 1990a: 214), as the Dearing Report (1993) testifies.

Poststructural feminism and educational politics

What such analyses show us about how curriculum discourses are produced and 'lived' is that inequalities and power relations are experienced and dealt with in very different ways (even by people from similar social groupings). Thus any solutions to inequality are likely to be complex. Poststructuralism suggests that the key to political action is in the 'critical' knowledges that people acquire about power. It is crucial, therefore, that feminist educators both maintain their critique of existing school practices and offer new challenges to meet the ever-changing circumstances of educational practice. Poststructuralism also points to a number of possibilities for feminist action in education: in particular, challenging the universalities and certainties of predominant curriculum epistemologies; adopting a feminist praxis and feminist pedagogical approaches which allow for possibilities of the expansion of feminist counter-discourses in education; and by the conscious positioning of feminist educators within educational practices.

First, as we have seen, feminist educators have considerable experience of collaborating with, and building on the work of, curriculum developers and academics in the creation of antisexist and non-discriminatory curricula. This work could be extended and inserted into current curriculum practices whether in school or in higher education, thus providing students with the possibility of engaging with a feminist critical counter-discourse. This might involve having to think 'creatively' (or dissidently), for example, by putting together sections of different curriculum units to create 'space' for students to pursue major enquiries into girls and women's lives and to explore the nature of patriarchal relations.

Practitioners will also need to develop *alternative* (feminist, antiracist and/or critical) pedagogical approaches to enable students to derive meaning from the various curricula offered to them. Students will then be more likely to see the importance and relevance of education in enabling them to take a more critical view of the academic 'truths' that they find in their curriculum texts. Pedagogical approaches might include adoption of materials-based or independent learning approaches, collaborative investigative work, or small group discussion of 'contentious' issues etc. Thus education could become a process of negotiation around curriculum and learning experiences, rather than the rote-learning of science in higher education or the perpetual round of tick-lists and assessment schedules of the present British classroom.

In their challenge to (as well as their 'delivery' of) the new curriculum, feminist educators will need to build on the feminist practices of collaboration and networking mentioned earlier, working with colleagues to develop and exchange a wide range of source materials. Curriculum development and institutional commitment (whether of school, college or university) to tackling educational inequalities will all be important. Collaboration and reciprocity with colleagues in different sectors of education is also likely to be valuable; in the development of appropriate teaching materials, or in order to extend professional skills or personal development, or for mutual support.

There is also potential for feminist educators within current educational practices. At policy level, feminist teachers mounting overtly political campaigns are likely to have greater impact by grouping together. To do this effectively, they will also need to develop accessible and plausible critiques of existing bodies of knowledge for discussion with colleagues and students or for publication in the educational press or journals. Given the increased power-base of schools, collaboration with parents and colleagues may lead to changes in school curricula or organization, if only at local level. The arrangement of seminars and conferences as means of exchanging information about developments in equality policies and practices in Britain and in other countries is likely to prove mutually supportive, and also encourage awareness that the educational practices which we are experiencing are not 'inevitable' or 'necessary' but derive from specific cultural, political and historical conditions which are continually shifting.

The most important insight that poststructuralism can offer women is a sense of our own power to live and to struggle. As Jones puts it,

a discursive construction of women and girls as powerful, as producing our own subjectivities *within and against* the 'spaces' provided *is* useful in offering more possibilities for women and girls to develop a wider range of practices.

(Jones 1993: 164)

In the next chapter I show how ideas within poststructuralism as well as within other feminisms have helped feminist educators explore and define the general characteristics of an ethical 'practice' grounded in feminism.

7

Developing a feminist praxis in pedagogy and research

Feminism has three main dimensions, political, critical and praxis-orientated – as I pointed out in Chapter 1. *Praxis* is a term that is used to signify the dialectical relationship between thought and action (or theory and practice) in certain 'practical sciences' such as teaching or nursing. It is viewed as a form of reasoning informed by action which, in a process of reflection on its character and consequences, is reflexively changed.

This chapter considers 'praxis' in the context of feminism, pedagogy and educational research for several reasons. First, as we have seen, feminism is a practice as well as a politics and value-system. Second, a number of philosophical critiques and perspectives have recently addressed the values underpinning and creating a praxis – critical theorists and feminists in particular. Third, as a feminist teacher in a higher education classroom, my personal, professional and micro-political relationships with students, the curriculum, colleagues and the institution in which I work, have been the focus of much reflection and self-reflection; in so doing, I have been drawn to the work developing in the United States and Australia on feminist pedagogy by people working in similar contexts to my own. Fourth, in various research studies with which

I have been involved, we have needed to address methodological and epistemological questions arising from what it has meant/ means to be a researcher of social justice issues in Britain in the 1980s and 1990s. The development of a form of feminist research praxis has seemed to be the inevitable outcome of developing an ethical practice in a feminist context (see, for example, Farish and Weiner 1992; Weiner 1992b). And finally, a bolder political point which I think needs to be made is that the development of a praxis for Left politics is long overdue. For a number of reasons, ironically given the numerous business and government scandals in the UK over recent years from the Guinness débâcle to the Iraq arms exposé to the spate of 'bedroom farces' in early 1994, the Right neverthe- less has maintained its hegemonic position over moral values. Thus its ethical posturing on issues such as law and order, discipline and standards, family values, the justice of the market and so on, has not only prospered but has seemed to relegate the Left to defend value positions often perceived as outdated and moribund. A new value position is in my view, therefore, urgently needed!

How are the relations of practice, theory and politics under- stood within feminism? Griffiths (1992) claims that all feminist epistemologies have a moral/political stance in which politics and values necessarily precede epistemology and in which facts are subordinated to values. Further, that feminism is not just about theory; it is about our everyday realities:

> There is a prevailing sexism in and out of formal educational institutions: schools, universities, local authorities, governing bodies, government departments, educational publishing and voluntary pressure groups. It distorts educational practices and educational outcomes. Inevitably it also distorts how we (all of us) understand ... them in order to improve them. This is precisely the concern of feminist epistemology: how to improve knowledge and remove sexist distortions.
>
> (Griffiths 1992: 3)

Developing a form of praxis suggested by such a moral/political stance of feminism and the difficulties in trying to achieve this in practice is the focus of this chapter. Thus I first explore the notion of praxis and how it can be conceptualized and extended, drawing also on ideas developed within feminist pedagogy and research. I then examine a particular instance of how feminist praxis was defined and constituted in a research project which examined how staff in higher education have been affected by institutional equal opportunities policies. The chapter concludes with some reflections about what use can be made of feminist and critical praxis more generally.

What is praxis?

The term *praxis* derives from Aristotle's notion that the practical arts of ethics, politics and education necessarily rest on knowledge which is uncertain and incomplete (Carr and Kemmis 1986). Later, Marx used the term as a means of contrasting action to philosophical speculation (Abercrombie *et al.* 1984) and this conceptualization was adopted and extended by Paulo Freire, in his work on liberation pedagogy which he developed when teaching adult literacy in South America. He conceptualized praxis as a fusion of subjectivity and objectivity in how people live out their lives:

> a process of orientation in the world [which] can be neither understood as a purely subjective event, nor as an objective or mechanistic one, but only as an event in which subjectivity and objectivity are united.
>
> (Freire 1972: 21)

Praxis, he argued, defines the interface between thought and action which constitutes the reality for most people. It is therefore crucial to the aspirations and decisions that shape their lives. As Weiler (1991) points out, Freire and feminists share a vision of social transformation and similar perspectives on oppression, consciousness and historical change. Thus:

> the ethical stance of Freire in terms of *praxis* and his articulation of people's worth and ability to know and change the world are an essential basis for radical pedagogy in opposition to oppression.
>
> (Weiler 1991: 455)

Interest in praxis in education was inspired also, in the late 1970s, by the pioneering work of Lawrence Stenhouse who sought to enhance the status of teachers by embedding their professionalism within a continual exercise of professional development focused on reflection and development of practice (Stenhouse 1975). Schon extended awareness and understanding of such terms as 'the reflective practitioner', 'teacher as researcher' and 'action research' in identifying teaching as a 'practical, applied science' which cannot easily be understood by the technical rationality of positivism. Instead, Schon (1987: ix) argues for a new epistemology of practice:

one that would stand the question of professional knowledge on its head by taking as its point of departure the competence and artistry already embedded in skilful practice – especially, the reflection-in-action (the 'thinking what they are doing' while they are doing it) that practitioners sometimes bring to situations of uncertainty, uniqueness and conflict.

In recognizing the importance of such 'artistry' in the improvement of professional practice, Schon compares this kind of knowledge to the privileged, systematic and scientific knowledge of the universities. He argues that there has been a crisis of confidence in professional education with a growing gap between high status scientific knowledge and what counts as professional knowledge and competence. What is overlooked, he contends, is the 'artistry', that is, the exercise of a kind of knowing, a tacit knowledge that is hard to put into words, at the core of the practice of every highly regarded professional (Schon 1987).

Beyond merely improving and valuing practice, the intimations of a more explicit Freirian political project are also evident within the mainstream praxis discourse. Stenhouse, for example, regarded teacher–research as potentially emancipatory in that it has the facility for liberating teachers and pupils from a system of education which denies individual dignity and is predicated on external authority and control. It also enables teachers rather than academics to develop educational theory grounded in classroom practice (Stenhouse, 1975). Thus within this discourse praxis is seen as informed action (of a 'teacher–researcher' or 'reflective practitioner') flowing from particular commitments in the light of particular circumstances and issues (Carr and Kemmis 1986). 'Critical praxis' goes one step further; it enables critical social scientists or practitioners to develop a practice that embraces their own political/ social values, beliefs and demands for change.

This [critical praxis] requires an integration of theory and practice as reflective and practical moments in a dialectic process of reflection, enlightenment and political struggle carried out by groups for the purpose of their own emancipation.

(Carr and Kemmis 1986: 144)

It follows, then, that involved as they are in political struggles for liberation and emancipation, feminists are ideally placed to adapt and integrate for their own purposes, concepts and practices derived from 'critical praxis'. However, in order to examine to what extent feminism has incorporated or developed ideas about critical praxis, we need also to understand how such ideas fit in with recent developments in feminist pedagogy and feminist educational research. These will be outlined (briefly) in the next sections.

Issues from feminist pedagogy

Interest in feminist pedagogy has arisen from concerns of feminist schoolteachers wishing to address gender issues in their classrooms and the parallel though not identical interests of feminist tutors involved in the expansion of Women's Studies programmes in North American colleges and universities. As Luke and Gore (1992: 8) point out, this work grew out of a growing discontent with the absence from pedagogical discourses of those discourses 'which proclaimed themselves as progressive and critical'. Thus attempts were made to argue for a pedagogy which was more centred on girls and women.

In posing the question 'what is feminist pedagogy?' Shrewsbury (1987) offers an unexpectedly conventional theory of teaching and learning which aims to guide the choice of pedagogical approach by linking criteria of evaluation to desired outcome. These evaluative criteria, however, also have a Freirian agenda.

> These evaluative criteria include the extent to which a community of learners is empowered to act responsibly toward one another and the subject matter and to apply learning to social action.
>
> (Shrewsbury, 1987, p. 6)

Weiler further argues that feminist pedagogy is concerned, in the main, with changing classroom methods to reflect three areas of concern: the role and authority of the teacher, the epistemological challenge of experience – 'the source of the claims for knowledge and truth in personal experience and feeling' (Weiler 1991: 459); and the emergent challenge of the new feminisms around questions of difference (specifically from women of colour and feminist postmodernism). Also, those committed to developing a feminist pedagogy have in common 'the goal of providing students with the skills to continue political work as feminists after they have left [education]' (Weiler 1991: 456) and to provide an alternative perspective and educational experience compared to those conventionally on offer.

The main problem, however, has been how to create critical consciousness without implying an ideological correctness or clashing with the complex desires and subjectivities of their female (and male) students. Taylor (1993) argues that feminist school-teachers need to take into account both students' resistance to feminism and the complex interplay of subjectivities in which femininity (and masculinity) is constructed, using them explicitly to develop a transformative pedagogy. She suggests specific strategies that would make the task possible including consciousness-raising; rendering the ordinary, extraordinary; helping girls to develop a collective sense of themselves as women and so on.

In a similar vein, but this time at university level, Magda Lewis undertook to challenge the backlash against feminism on campus by creating a feminist pedagogy that is celebratory as well as critical:

> that supports women's desire to wish well for ourselves when for many women 'good news' of the transformative powers of feminist consciousness turns into the 'bad news' of social inequality and, therefore, a perspective and politics they want to resist.
>
> (Lewis 1990: 468)

Specifically, Lewis treats the psychological, social and sexual dynamics of the feminist classroom as a site where the political struggle over meaning can be viewed as part of a project involving women in examining and questioning self-consciously to 'develop a critical understanding' in order to work towards a conscious transformation (Lewis 1990: 469). Further, Lewis identifies 'pedagogical moments' as arising in specific contexts when all the elements affecting the classroom come together 'in ways that create the specifics of the moment'; these elements may include the social location of the teacher and students, the political climate in which they work, the personalities and profiles of individuals in the classroom and so on. Lewis uses these moments, which she sees as transformative in enabling greater understandings of the gendered context of the classroom, to develop 'an interpretive framework for creating a counter-hegemony' (Lewis 1990: 487); in other less overtly political discourses, these 'moments' may well be termed 'critical incidents' or 'illuminating instances'.

As Lewis also points out, the urgency of developing a feminist pedagogy arises from the presence of feminist teachers and their commitment to a conscious reflection on their practice, in particular, how it relates to in/equalities in power relations, the encouragement to critical thinking in students and the living out of values in practice. So, here, feminist pedagogy emerges as a specific form of feminist praxis:

> The challenge of feminist teaching lies for me in the specifics of how I approach the classroom. By reflecting on my own teaching, I fuse content and practice, politicizing them both through feminist theory and living them both concretely, rather than treating them abstractly.
>
> (Lewis 1990: 485)

Feminism and research

As we saw in Chapter 4, feminism has been viewed as a paradigm of modernity and as such, many feminists have been content to work within modernist research conventions at the same time as attempting to place the social construction of gender at the centre of their enquiry (Hekman 1990; Griffiths 1992; Weiner 1992b). Yet, as we have also seen, feminism has played a vanguard role in challenging science's epistemological foundations which are rooted in modernity, by anticipating (and engaging with) many of the recent debates arising from poststructuralism and postmodernism. Thus challenges have been made to universal, patriarchal, research paradigms, i.e. the study of 'man' (e.g. Stanley and Wise 1983); positivism's claim to neutrality and objectivity (e.g. Harding 1987); the distortion and invisibility of the female experience (Smith 1978); the notion of the autonomous and rational individual as the main goal of education (Walkerdine 1990); the extent to which educational research itself can challenge inequality (Weiner 1990); and arguments put forward about the shifting category of 'woman' as outlined in the poststructural writing of Weedon (1987) and Riley (1988) and so on.

More specifically, feminist researchers have concentrated as much on the 'how', the practice of research, as on findings and knowledge-claims. For example, Oakley (1981), and the authors in the influential *Theories of Women's Studies* collection (Bowles and Duelli Klein 1983) reject positivist 'cold' approaches of the 'scientific' method in favour of more interactive, contextualized methods both to improve the experience for women of being researched and 'in search of pattern and meaning rather than for prediction and control' (Lather 1991: 72). This, in turn, has led to questions, for example, about power relations within the research process (Riddell 1989), the necessary reflexivity of the researcher (Lather 1991) and the need for feminist emphasis on the importance of subjectivity and personal involvement in the research process (Stanley and Wise 1990).

It is also clear, however, that there is no one inclusive feminist research method and in fact, feminism itself is a site of struggle over meaning (for a discussion of the disagreements and contradictions within feminism, see Hirsch and Fox Keller 1990). Nevertheless, as has already been pointed out, embedded in feminist research as a form of praxis is a concern about the practices and processes of research (and this is where it differs from the work of Stenhouse and Schon) which also engages with social justice/injustice, from a vantage point which may be viewed as more (or differently) illuminating than other vantage points (see Harding 1990, and also Hill Collins 1990, for discussion of a black, feminist vantage point). Further, Smith argues that standpoint theory has crucial cultural as well as empirical consequences for women by: 'taking up the standpoint of women as an experience of being, of society, of social and personal process which must be given form and expression within the culture' (Smith 1978: 294). Although currently popular, standpoint theory nevertheless has drawn criticism since it is quite obvious that certain feminist standpoints, for example, those of white, academic, middle-class feminists, have clear predominance over others such as the 'silenced feminist standpoints' of black and lesbian feminist epistemology (Stanley and Wise 1990).

Identifying feminist praxis

What might a feminist praxis look like, then, which draws on the debates arising out of feminism, pedagogy and research; that includes the full range of women (feminists?) involved in education whether as teachers, researchers, academics, parents, administrators etc; and that is applicable to the various contexts of education, from the primary classroom to the university lecture theatre? What might a feminist praxis look like that, in drawing on the work of Freire, Schon, Stenhouse, Carr and Kemmis, Lather and Stanley, also embodies the moral/political stance of feminism suggested by Griffiths?

Patti Lather uses praxis as an organizing principle of feminist pedagogy and research. For Lather, 'praxis is the self-creative activity through which we make the world . . . it is *the* central concept of a philosophy that did not want to remain a philosophy, philosophy becoming practical' (1991: 11). Drawing on Gramsci's appeal for adherence to a praxis of the present, Lather argues that it should illuminate the lived experiences of progressive or oppressed groups and itself should be illuminated by their struggles. She also suggests that praxis requires both 'reciprocity' as a means of consciously empowering those involved to change their situation and 'reflexivity' as a means of progressing critical enquiry. Thus it seems that feminist praxis constitutes a fusion of values, theoretical perspectives and practice with a specific grounding in feminist epistemology.

This fusion is visible in Stanley's (1990) broader use of the term more to connect three themes within feminist research. First, praxis constitutes an indication of a continuing feminist commitment to changing the world rather than merely researching it; the term should not, however, be used as a signifier for one particular feminist position (Stanley criticizes Lather for applying praxis exclusively to action research). Second, praxis rejects the 'theory/research' divide, uniting 'manual and intellectual activities which are symbiotically related' (Stanley 1990: 15). Third, it dissolves the methodological/epistemological split in which 'method' is the relatively insignificant 'how' subordinated to the significant 'what' – the knowledge that is being sought. Here, then, the vision of feminist praxis is further extended to encompass not only theory, action and values but also has the epistemological aim of challenging and dissolving conventional, regulative dualisms such as male–female, mental–manual, black–white, theory–practice and so on.

In fact, from the earliest days of modern feminism, demands for change involved praxis issues: for instance, calling for the 'personal as political', namely expecting people to live out their overtly egalitarian political values in private as well as in public life or for the development of 'woman-friendly' non-hierarchical and non-conflictual settings and practices. How to act on inequalities in power relationships has also been viewed as an important element of feminist practice, as is usefully illustrated in the recent debate in the United States about how differences within feminism can be questioned without resorting to the conflictual male academic model of attack, defence, counter-attack etc. In particular, concerns were expressed about how different feminists may be positioned within such a discourse:

> Feminists have a lot of trouble with our own authority [that of senior academic women] because women are still not generally in power. If we hold to a general [feminist] perspective we are still powerless victims oppressed as women. But if we talk about the world in which we operate, the small academic world of literary criticism, feminists do have power.
>
> (Gallop *et al.* 1990: 354)

Quite clearly, then, the demands of a feminist, critical praxis are likely to be numerous, complex and highly contested, though this should not detract from any attempts to develop one. Moreover, it will certainly contain some, if not all, of the following features:

- deriving from experience and rooted in practice;
- continually subject to revision as a result of experience;
- reflexive and self-reflexive;
- widely accessible and open to change;
- grounded in the analysis of women's (and men's) multiple and different material realities;
- illuminative of women's (and men's) multiple and different experiences and material realities;
- explicitly political and value-led;
- within the classroom, imbued with feminist organizational practices grounded in equality, non-hierarchy and democracy;
- within educational research, additionally rejecting conventional dualisms such as theory/practice, mental/manual, epistemology/methodology.

Developing a feminist research praxis

I have attempted, thus far, to discuss how the notion of feminist praxis has been treated within the classroom, within research and within feminism generally. In this section I want to show how the concern to develop a feminist ethics or praxis shaped the method, organization and analysis of a particular project with which I was involved whose main aim was to explore the 'practice' of equal opportunities policy in colleges and universities. In particular I focus on the concerns of members of the project team about their own research practice in the context of ideas about feminist *praxis* as outlined above.[1] The project was not without its problems – illness of team members, lack of resources, difficulties of liaison with case-study institutions, occasional differences of perspective between project team members and so on – but it is my view that the careful reflections on the research process at the onset of the project gave us a framework for dealing with each problem as it arose.

Briefly, the project which started in November 1991 and was completed in March 1994, had the determinedly *social justice* brief of promoting greater equity for staff in colleges and universities. It involved detailed and longitudinal (two-year) case-studies of three educational institutions, one each from the further education (vocational college), new university (ex-polytechnic) and traditional university sectors. A variety of research methods were used including formal and group interviews; informal conversations and dialogues; questionnaires; documentary analyses; observation of events, people, meetings and buildings; staff audits; and, in two cases, tracking the senior manager. The project's chosen methodology – the policy case-study – seemed to rest easily within the feminist research paradigm in that it was multi-method and anti-positivist, aiming to be interactive and reciprocal, attentive to subjectivities, potentially flexible and richly descriptive.

In an early project paper, Maureen Farish and I argued for the adoption of a multi-theory, multi-method approach to the project (drawing on 'grounded theory', 'case study', 'organizational theory' and 'feminist epistemology') (Farish and Weiner 1992). However feminist epistemology appeared to be most crucial of the methodological approaches to the investigation and implementation of equal opportunities, in allowing possibilities for both the promotion of greater equality and recognition of differences. The concern of the researchers about the principles of ethical practice led us to focus on a number of different issues: in particular, composition of the project team, project organization, reflexivity and reciprocity of the research process, analysis and presentation of findings.

We also realized that praxis demanded greater explicitness about the research process rather than the relatively greater emphasis, conventionally, on findings and resultant contribution to knowledge.

The project team

The research team comprised four white women from various ethnic backgrounds, at different levels in academia and of different ages and stages in their lives and careers. Two of us worked at South Bank University in London and two at the Scottish Council for Research in Education in Edinburgh, Scotland. None of us was full-time as the project was relatively low-funded (approximately £40,000 over 30 months) but the fact that the project work was spread across the four of us meant that we felt able to share perspectives, interests, decisions and responsibilities, and also to provide 'cover' for other project members where necessary.

The principles of feminist research were seen by us as applicable to forms of humanist research relating to groups other than women. Thus, by adopting a 'feminist standpoint' for the project which recognizes differences between women, it also provided the framework for the recognition of differences within and between other social groupings. As Cockburn (1989: 10) notes:

> Men tell us 'women cannot claim to be equal if they are different from men. You have to choose'. We now have a reply. If we say, as women, we can be both the same as you *and* different from you, at various times and in various ways. We can also be the same and different from each other. What we are seeking is not in fact *equality* but *equivalence*, not *sameness* for individual women and men but *parity* for women as a sex, or for groups of women in their specificity.

We were conscious, however, that as white women, the researchers represented one main segment of underrepresentation (due to the unintended exclusion of black researchers from the project team because of the structural racism of the contract research process). We aimed to redress this imbalance by having a more representative project advisory group and also by being particularly alert to issues of 'race' and ethnicity and other forms of inequality in our research practice. However, we were also conscious of the significance of the absence of a black feminist standpoint from our research.

Project organization

The structure of the project was designed to be relatively flat and non-hierarchical, though, inevitably, status differences between project members could not entirely be eradicated. As the project director, I took main responsibility for general administration including organizing project meetings, writing and distributing minutes and taking any necessary follow-up action. I was also responsible for the overall smooth running of the project, filling any pressing gaps in the fieldwork. Each of the other researchers (Maureen Farish, Joanna McPake and Janet Powney) had the main responsibility for one of the case-studies and also played a 'minor' role in a second case-study, taking a share of the fieldwork and having some familiarity with the specific institutional context.

In the course of the project, as might be expected, several of the researchers had a period of time away from the project. The collaborative nature of the project organization worked well at these times in that it allowed for researchers to cover for each other but also to 'slow down' the pace of the research to accommodate any relatively short-term absences or problems. Maintaining a reasonable level of communication between members of the research team was also a significant factor in the project organization since the case-study institutions and our own institutional bases are relatively geographically dispersed, the researchers sometimes worked from home and all had other professional and personal responsibilities and commitments. Also travel funds were severely limited therefore communication between the researchers necessarily needed to be flexible and continuous. However, by exploiting relatively recent developments in communication technologies, we managed to maintain regular contact through the telephone (for individual calls and regular 'formal' telephone conferences), the fax and termly face-to-face meetings in London or Edinburgh.

Research process

Initially, access to the case-study institutions was negotiated with the senior management, though the research team were conscious of the pitfalls (and advantages) of such a top-down research entry. Some degree of 'protection' for both researchers and staff from the case-study institutions was gained, however, through agreement to 'ethical guidelines' involving access to information, opportunities to respond and amend research accounts and guaranteed anonymity, where possible. Thus, all research accounts were returned to appropriate staff members to check for meaning and accuracy.

Nevertheless, it became apparent fairly early on that in some instances, the project was being used by institutions as part of their agenda-setting and public relations objectives. Also, some interviewees and respondents revealed their anxiety and feelings of vulnerability concerning their own institutional positioning by the manner in which they scrutinized the research accounts, eradicating any perceived contentious statements. Certainly, in one case, statements about the difficulties for gay members of staff were eliminated from an interview account, generating much discussion in the research team about who had ultimate control over the research data. We questioned, for instance, whether, it is ethical *in all instances* for an interviewee to retain control over the research account!

Different research approaches were replicated across institutions: for example, those of tracking a senior manager, following through the staff recruitment process and distributing a questionnaire eliciting the response of the main body of staff to equal opportunity policy-making. The intention was not to compare policies and practices within institutions which have very different histories and cultures, but rather to seek understanding through the prism of difference.

Analysis

A common problem with collecting data drawn from a wide range of sources and by a variety of methods is how to develop a coherent and plausible analysis: that is, what to do with the data that sits there 'sprawling, diffuse, undefined and diverse' (Loflund, quoted in Lather 1991: 124). Although the main form of analysis was to organize and present the data as case-studies, we drew on other research studies of equal opportunities policy-making (Cockburn 1989, 1991; Jenkins and Solomos 1989; Faludi 1991) to build a more analytic framework around certain key points. These include:

• *disappointment* – in the failure of previous policies relating to equal opportunities;

- *difference/specificity* – of groups, institutions, individuals, contexts, agendas, cultures;
- *resistance* – or 'backlash', of groups, individuals to equal opportunities policies;
- *contradiction* – in interpretation of equal opportunities and between institutional imperatives and staff cultures;
- *universalizing tendencies* – of policies which see subordinate groups as homogeneous, for example, being devised to suit all women or only black staff (or in research terms, claiming that feminist understanding is sufficient to understand the position of other oppressed groups);
- *power relations* – in policy-making, between management and main-grade staff, and in the research process, e.g. between white researchers and black respondents, or between low status (female) researchers and high status (male) respondents.

One way of taking the above elements into account in the analysis was to focus on the specifics of a 'moment' in the research, adapting Lewis's powerful notion of a 'pedagogical moment' (see page 126) and drawing also on case-study methodology as a means of using multiple sources of evidence to focus on an instance (Hakim 1987). The attempt was made to bring together feminist values, theory and practice within feminist praxis in order to create new analytical practices and critical meanings which could, nevertheless, be applied more generally:

> as a way of analysing how they [discursive practices] are structured, what power relations they produce and reproduce, where there are resistances and where we might look for weak points more open to challenge and transformation.
> (Weedon 1987: 137)

Utilizing the moment!

One such 'moment', which will now be discussed in some detail, involved four individual interviews on staff perceptions of equal opportunity policy, taking place on the same wet and windy day in May in the same higher education institution. The interviews were arranged by the main case-study researcher who gained access to staff via the Dean of Faculty. Another member of the research team did the interviewing using a semi-structured interview schedule covering knowledge of, and involvement and sympathy with, the institution's equal opportunities policy. The interviewees were sent a copy of the questions prior to their interview.

The variety of possible classifications of the interviewees serves to reveal the potentiality for 'fragmentation' of the research subject. For example, all the interviewees were white; two were relatively high status (male dean [H], female professor [J]) and two relatively low status (male, semi-retired part-time lecturer [K], young, female research assistant [L]); two were male (H & K) and two female (J and L); two were long-established staff members (H and K) and two were relatively new (J and L); one (L) was much younger than the other three etc.

The interviews took place in the interviewees' rooms or rooms of their own choosing. All seemed willing to be interviewed, were polite and, though having cleared time to be interviewed, were clearly busy. What is evident from the field-notes is that each interviewee, rather than reveal any hidden 'truth' or new perspective, appeared swiftly to take up a position, to 'claim an identity' (Maclure 1993), in relation to equal opportunities and in relation to the university.

Thus, K (male, part-time lecturer) identified himself both as a long-time staff member and having views typical of the institution as a whole – though he felt perhaps that he was rather more advanced in his thinking compared with some of his colleagues in the all-male department in which he works. According to the field-notes:[2]

> K would think that his view on equal opportunities is shared by the University, and [he] is fairly comfortable with the current EO policy . . . in the main most staff have been fairly indifferent . . . While changes have occurred, there are lecturers who are less open to influence than K. But then, K is probably less responsive than he would like to be.

In contrast, L (female, research assistant) portrayed herself as quite angry, in particular, about the day-to-day behaviour of colleagues and would like more done about the 'jocular' sexist remarks of male colleagues whereby 'points are still scored and the "correct" message sent' and understood! She felt herself to be already 'way ahead of the language guidelines provided' and expressed disappointment in her lack of involvement in equal opportunities policy-making. She identified most with being female, young and on a temporary contract; so overall, though 'L regards herself as receptive and interested in any development' her conclusions about the university equal opportunities policy was that it is 'disappointing'.

H presented himself as a well respected, hard working and long-standing member of the university with a good research record. He was very aware of the 'still very powerful senior management and lay individuals who are instinctively rather than intellectually opposed to EO. Most can deal with women on court only if they can flirt . . . [they] cannot cope with those who "talk back"'. Yet H managed to help ease or 'nod through' official policy and support the activities of various feminists in his faculty. He was the only one of those interviewed to provide an overview of how equal opportunities had developed over the years – as a result of the variable efforts of the three university principals. For instance, he remembered that the 'gender specific language booklet created real "rage" among some lay members of court'. H reasoned that though considerable progress has been made by the university, there were still major problems and 'it is still not taken as seriously as it should be'.

Finally, J (recently appointed, female professor) appeared to have the most sophisticated and knowledgeable perception of the strengths and limitations of the institution's equal opportunities policy. She reported that though there seemed to be little overt discrimination against women, there were only three female professors, no female heads of department or deans and no women in the senior management group. There was also no thorough-going support of equal opportunities, no proper monitoring, and no attempt made to ensure female representation on the important university committees: 'thus women have no purchase over resource allocation'. Moreover the university culture was strongly male, middle-aged, and middle-class.

Despite this catalogue of poor practice and 'want of a system', J did not appear as angry as L – perhaps because she had moved, at least to some degree, through the 'glass ceiling' and was less vulnerable to the day-to-day sexism of male colleagues. As to her view on the university's equal opportunities policy, she intimated that there was a degree of smugness at higher levels: 'It's a bit of a "curate's egg". There are some good things happening but the university still has a long way to go.'

Analysing the specifics of the moment

This 'moment' focuses on the receivers and interpreters of equal opportunities policy in one higher education institution. What is noticeable in the interviews of K (part-time lecturer) and L (research assistant) is how 'in the dark' about policy they were compared with H (male dean) and J (female professor). Thus, the interviewees' knowledge of policy, their support of and resistance, their identification with and criticism of policy, all seemed closely related to their immediate professional and personal contexts – and to their multiple realities. The two female interviewees would, no doubt, have identified themselves as feminists, if asked. Yet their perception of the policy and its actual (or potential) impact on their immediate circumstances, their bargaining power in the market place, their differential positioning in the power–knowledge practices within the policy discourse of their institution, all served to highlight their differences rather than their shared interests. However, their shared experience of sexist practices enabled them to offer a sharper perspective on the 'problem' of inequality than their male colleagues.

The two male interviewees, in contrast, portrayed themselves as more detached, more 'rational', more distanced from equal opportunities concerns. They both suggested that it was vociferous feminists in their faculty and outside the university who had raised the stakes and/or created the fuss. They, themselves, seemed somehow frozen on the sidelines, able to act only in offering or withdrawing their support. Further, whilst H appeared to have a genuine commitment to enhancing equality within the university, it seemed to be related more to altruism than to any deeply felt passion for challenging existing practices or material conditions that might affect *him*.

In fact, what most united the two male interviewees was their concern to dismiss 'positive action' – it was not mentioned by either of the female interviewees. In K's case, though he acknowledged that discrimination goes on (and, indeed, provided examples), he asserted his absolute opposition to any positive action strategies in favour of women. In H's case, while he articulated a sympathy for positive action, his insistence that there would be insufficient support for it to have any chance of being adopted as university policy has similar implications. 'Positive action', possibly the most 'radical' of the policies available, thus, was used ritually by the men as a signifier for marking the boundaries of equal opportunity policy-making.

This 'moment', it is hoped, serves to show how the adoption of a poststructural feminist standpoint for the analysis enabled the identification of the specifics that underlie policy and practice in a patriarchal society while at the same time allowing for differences, other than gender, also to have significance.

Presentation of findings

There were a number of stages through which the findings of the project passed in order to enter the public domain: accounts were written up, sent back to those involved to check for accuracy and meaning, incorporated into regular report-backs to the case-study institutions and to various advisory groups, and incorporated into academic papers and the final report. Overall the main aims of the project were to get to some sort of 'truth' about the policy-making process and to enhance the effectiveness of those attempting to promote greater equality. So clearly, the manner in which we framed the report-backs was important, and indeed was carefully discussed beforehand. For example, were we going to be challenging or congratulatory, critical or sympathetic? Were we going to play the naïve researcher or the seasoned academic? Most of all, what we sought from the institutions involved in the study was to win them over to a more highly prioritized commitment to equality and, through the research data provided on their institution, to help them explore how they could best move forward.

In fact, though there were illuminating and cheering exceptions, the patterns that we found and reported were depressingly familiar: for example, a predominance of staffing structures with exclusively (white) male chief executives, senior management including some women but few black staff, women more likely to have main responsibilities and posts for equal opportunities rather than being in the key 'power' positions of senior management etc. Moreover, those women (black or white) who had achieved senior positions suffered from feelings of visibility and isolation, hostility from (male) subordinates and sometimes from colleagues, patronizing behaviour from their bosses, overload and overwork, and continually being viewed as the abnormal 'Other' – or just simply not 'one of the boys'. At the same time, there seemed to be a continual need to revise and update policy initiatives, intimations of a backlash waiting to be unleashed and problems (and possibilities) arising from the multiple positioning of staff members in relation to equality issues – often simultaneously supportive and resistant.

An added difficulty was that the two-year period in which we conducted the research was one of immense and continual change across all the sectors represented by the case-study institutions. Instigated by the British government policy orientated towards the market, the case-study institutions experienced amalgamations, important changes in status, institutional name-changes, internal restructuring and reorganization, resultant relocation of work and office space and so on. Thus, while the project, in the main, was welcomed by those working in the institutions involved, equality as a policy issue was viewed as on the move *down* rather than up the policy agenda.

Is this feminist praxis?

In attempting to articulate a feminist research praxis, I have considered the emergence of the notion of praxis within education, and attempted to envisage a feminist praxis, drawing on recent discussions within feminist research and feminist pedagogy. In accordance with the explicit requirement within praxis of 'openness' and 'reflexivity' I have also provided some detail on the structure and organization of a particular research study, with which I have been involved, in order to expose its praxis orientation.

Did our practice as researchers meet the requirements of a feminist research *praxis*? Was it characterized by the following: *greater explicitness* about the research process, for instance, concerning organizational arrangements, how decisions are made, the theoretical and methodological frameworks used etc.; *evidence of reflexivity and self-reflexivity* of researchers and a willingness to be open to criticism; *flexibility* of research methodology based on some form of reflection on practice; existence of a *feminist consciousness*, and in particular, of a clear understanding of the implicit and explicit power relations within the research team, between the researcher and the researched, and within institutional research contexts?

Was indeed feminist praxis achieved? Perhaps this is an impossible question to answer since, to quote hooks, feminist thought is always on the move as a 'theory in the making' (hooks 1984: 10). Perhaps in this case intention is more important, or at least as important, as outcome. Moreover, other 'critical' researchers might claim sympathy with most of the tenets of feminist praxis and research. The point to make here is that whatever the outcome, feminist thought and consciousness helped us to shape our practice. Thus, the aims of the researchers were to be *reflexive* in our concerns about black non-representation on the research team, in the way we worked together, and in our relations with the case-study institutions. We also tried to respond to themes emerging from the data in shaping how we collected the data and the forms of analysis we chose. Thus we attempted to reveal the *hierarchies* at play and to make 'resistant discourses' more widely heard and available – for the explicit purpose, as Lather (1991) puts it, of interrupting power imbalances. We tried to portray the complex interplay of *power relations* – in the knowledge that a rather more simplistic analysis would have been more welcome from the policy-makers in our study.

Clearly there was also a micropolitics about how we, as researchers, presented our case. Thus, how project accounts were written explicitly and implicitly foregrounded certain values and biases (see for example, Farish and Weiner 1992; McPake 1992; Powney 1992) and of course, for all the project team, this research was part of our paid work and a 'shop-window' for future employment and career progress.

However, whether we have become better researchers or more conscious of social justice issues (though these are of course important) may be of less interest ultimately than whether the project helped to change things at the macro and micro-political levels of the case-study institutions, and more widely – a much more difficult (if not impossible) evaluation task.

As to the more grandiose goal of contributing to the development of a 'praxis of the Left', and this perhaps can stand as the concluding remark for the book, I can do no more than (perhaps, presumptuously) suggest a way forward based on the previous discussion of educational praxis which, nevertheless, arises out of a specific progressive politics – that of feminism. In my view, drawing from the debates within feminism (as well as within other critical movements) a new values position and praxis could well benefit from greater emphasis on and exploration of the following four elements:

- social justice/equality concerns at *micro* as well as macro-political levels;

- the importance of changing *practice* as well as structures;
- the *complexities* of human experience which render relations of dominance/subordination as more problematic than in the past;
- the necessity of greater *openness* and the need to be *responsive* to changing circumstances and demands.

Notes

1 The research team for the Equity and Staffing Project (funded by the FSRC, no. R000 23 3301) comprised Janet Powney and Joanna McPake from the Scottish Council for Research in Education and Maureen Farish and Gaby Weiner from South Bank University.
2 All the field-notes and accounts of interviews quoted here were checked and validated by the main project participants and interviewees.

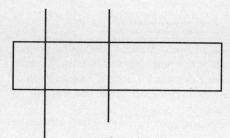

References

Abercrombie, N., Hill, S. and Turner, B.S. (1984) *The Penguin Dictionary of Sociology.* Harmondsworth, Penguin.

Acker, S. (1986) What feminists want from education. In Hartnett, A. and Naish, M. (eds) *Education and Society Today.* London, Falmer Press.

Adler, S., Laney, J. and Packer, M. (1993) *Managing Women.* Buckingham, Open University Press.

Amos, V. and Parmar, P. (1984) Challenging imperial feminism, *Feminist Review*, 17: 3–18.

Anyon, J. (1979) Ideology and United States history textbooks, *Harvard Educational Review*, 49 (3): 361–86.

Apple, M.W. (1986) *Teachers and Texts: A Political Economy of Class and Gender Relations in Education.* New York, Routledge & Kegan Paul.

Apple, M.W. and Christian Smith, L. (eds) (1991) *The Politics of the Textbook.* London, Routledge.

Arnot, M. (1987) Political lip-service or radical reform? Central Government responses to sex equality as a policy issue. In Arnot, M. and Weiner, G. (eds) *Gender and the Politics of Schooling.* London, Hutchinson.

Arnot, M. (1992) Feminism, education and the New Right. In Arnot, M. and Barton, L. (eds) *Voicing Concerns: Sociological Perspectives on Contemporary Education Reforms.* Oxford, Triangle Books.

Arnot, M. (1993) A crisis in patriarchy? British feminist educational politics and state regulation of gender. In Arnot, M. and Weiler, K. (eds) *Feminism and Social Justice in Education*. London, Falmer Press.

Arnot, M. and Weiner, G. (eds) (1987) *Gender and the Politics of Schooling*. London, Hutchinson.

Avent, C. (1982) Careers education and guidance, *Secondary Education Journal*, 12 (2): 6–7.

Ball, S.J. (1990a) *Politics and Policy Making in Education*. London, Routledge.

Ball, S.J. (1990b) Introducing Monsieur Foucault. In Ball, S.J. (ed.) *Foucault and Education: Disciplines and Knowledge*. London, Routledge.

Ball, S.J. (1990c) Management as moral technology: A Luddite analysis. In Ball, S.J. (ed.) *Foucault and Education: Disciplines and Knowledge*. London, Routledge.

Banks, O. (1968) *Sociology of Education*. London, Fletcher & Sons.

Banks, O. (1981) *Faces of Feminism*. Oxford, Martin Robertson.

Barrett, M. (1980) *Women's Oppression Today: Problems in Marxist Feminist Analysis*. London, Verso.

Bernstein, B. (1971) On the classification and framing of educational knowledge. In Young, M. (ed.) *Knowledge and Control*. London, Collier-Macmillan.

Blackmore, J. (1992) *Making Educational History: A Feminist Perspective*. Geelong, Deakin University.

Bloom, B. (ed.) (1956) *Taxonomy of Educational Objectives*. London, Longman.

Board of Education (1923) *Report of the Consultative Committee on the Differentiation of the Curriculum for Boys and Girls*. London, HMSO.

Bouchier, D. (1983) *The Feminist Challenge*. London, Macmillan.

Bowlby, J. (1953) *Child Care and the Growth of Love*. Harmondsworth, Penguin.

Bowles, G. and Duelli Klein, R. (eds) (1983) *Theories of Women's Studies*. London, Routledge & Kegan Paul.

Brah, A. and Minhas, R. (1985) Structural racism or cultural difference: Schooling for Asian girls. In Weiner, G. (ed.) *Just a Bunch of Girls: Feminist Approaches to Schooling*. Milton Keynes, Open University Press.

Brownmiller, S. (1975) *Against Our Will: Men, Women and Rape*. New York, Simon & Schuster.

Bruner, J. (1960) *Process of Education*. Cambridge, MA, Harvard University Press.

Bruner, J. (1966) *Towards a Theory of Instruction*. New York, Macmillan.

Bryan, B., Dadzie, S. and Scafe, S. (1985) *The Heart of the Race: Black Women's Lives in Britain*. London, Virago.

Burchell, H. (1989) Strategies for change in new initiatives. In Burchell, H. and Millman, V. (eds) *Changing Perspectives on Gender: New Initiatives in Secondary Education*. Milton Keynes, Open University Press.

Burton, L. and Weiner, G. (1990) Social Justice and the National Curriculum, *Research Papers in Education*, 5 (3): 203–28.

Calinescu, M. (1985) Introductory remarks. In Calinescu, M. and Fokkema, D. (eds) *Exploring Postmodernism*. Amsterdam, John Benjamins Publishing Company.

Carby, H. (1987) Black feminism and the boundaries of sisterhood. In Arnot, M. and Weiner, G. (eds) *Gender and the Politics of Schooling*. London, Hutchinson.

Carr, W. (1993) Reconstructing the curriculum debate: An editorial introduction, *Curriculum Studies*, 1 (1): 5–9.

Carr, W. and Kemmis, S. (1986) *Becoming Critical: Education, Knowledge and Action Research*. London, Falmer Press.

Castell, S., Luke, A. and Luke, C. (1989) *Language, Authority and Criticism*. London, Falmer Press.

Central Advisory Council for Education in England (1963) *Half Our Future* [the Newsom Report]. London, HMSO.

Central Advisory Council for Education in England (1967) *Children in their Primary Schools* [the Plowden Report]. London, HMSO.

Chisholm, L. and Holland, J. (1987) Anti-sexist action research in schools: the Girls and Occupational Choice Project. In Weiner, G. and Arnot, M. (eds) *Gender Under Scrutiny*. London, Hutchinson.

Chodorow, N. (1978) *The Reproduction of Mothering: Psychoanalysis and the Sociology of Gender*. Berkeley, University of California Press.

Christian Smith, L. (ed.) (1993) *Texts of Desire: Girls, Popular Fiction and Education*. London, Falmer Press.

Cixous, H. (1971) Sorties. In Marks, E. and de Courtivron, I. (eds) *New French Feminisms*. New York, Schocken Books.

Clanchy, J. (1993) Terse but not to the point, *Times Educational Supplement*, 5 March.

Clarricoates, K. (1978) Dinosaurs in the classroom – A re-examination of some aspects of the 'hidden curriculum' in primary schools, *Women's Studies International Quarterly*, 1: 353–64.

Clift, P., Weiner, G. and Wilson, E. (1983) *Record-Keeping in the Primary School*. London, Macmillan.

Cockburn, C. (1989) Equal opportunities: The long and short agenda, *Industrial Relations Journal*, Autumn.

Cockburn, C. (1991) *In the Way of Women: Men's Resistance to Sex Equality in Organisations*. London, Macmillan.

Committee of the Secondary Schools Examinations Council (1943) *Curriculum and Examinations in Secondary Schools* [the Norwood Report]. London, HMSO.

Connell, R.W. (1989) Cool guys, swots and wimps: The interplay of masculinity and education, *Oxford Review of Education*, 15 (3): 291–303.

Cornbleet, A. and Libovitch, S. (1983) Anti-sexist initiatives in a mixed comprehensive school: A case study. In Wolpe, A. and Donald, J. (eds) *Is There Anyone Here from Education?* London, Pluto Press.

Daly, M. (1979) *Gyn/Ecology*. London, The Women's Press.

David, M. (1980) *The State, the Family and Education*. London, Routledge & Kegan Paul.

Davies, B. and Banks, C. (1992) The gender trap: A feminist post-structuralist analysis of primary school children's talk about gender, *Journal of Curriculum Studies*, 24 (1): 1–25.

Davies, B. (1989) *Frogs and Snails and Feminist Tales: Pre-school Children and Gender*. Sydney, Allen & Unwin.

Davis, A. (1981) *Women, Race and Class*. London, The Women's Press.

Dawes, L. (1992) Gender and Curriculum Policy in the Australian Context. Unpublished doctoral thesis, University of Queensland.

Dean, D. (1991) Education for moral improvement, domesticity and social cohesion: Expectations and fears of the Labour Government, *Oxford Review of Education*, 17 (3): 269–85.

Dearing, R. (1993) *The National Curriculum and its Assessment: Final Report* [the Dearing Report]. London, Schools Curriculum and Assessment Authority.

de Beauvoir, S. (1953) *The Second Sex*, trans. and ed. H.M. Parshley. London, Jonathan Cape.

Deem, R. (ed.) (1980) *Schooling for Women's Work*. London, Routledge & Kegan Paul.

Deem, R. (1981) State policy and ideology in the education of women, *British Journal of Sociology of Education*, 2 (2): 131–43.

Deem, R. (ed.) (1984) *Coeducation Reconsidered*. Milton Keynes, Open University Press.

Delamont, S. and Duffin, L. (eds) (1978) *The Nineteenth-Century Woman: Her Cultural and Physical World*. London, Croom Helm.

Delmar, R. (1986) What is feminism? In Mitchell, J. and Oakley, A. (eds) *What is Feminism?* Oxford, Basil Blackwell.

Delphy, C. (1980) A material feminism is possible, *Feminist Review*, 4: 79–98.

Department of Education and Science (DES) (1989a) *The Education Reform Act 1988: The School Curriculum and Assessment: Circular 5/89*. London, HMSO.

Department of Education and Science (DES) (1989b) *National Curriculum: From Policy to Practice*. London, HMSO.

Dewey, J. (1966) The child and the curriculum. In Garforth, F.W. (ed.) *John Dewey: Selected Educational Writings*. London, Heinemann.

Dinnerstein, D. (1976) *The Mermaid and the Minotaur: Sexual Arrangements and Human Malaise.* New York, Harper & Row.

Dworkin, A. (1981) *Pornography: Men Possessing Women.* New York, Perigree Books.

Eddowes, M. (1983) *Humble-pi: The Mathematics Education of Girls.* York, Longman.

Faludi, S. (1991) *Backlash: The Undeclared War Against Women.* London, Chatto & Windus.

Farish, M. and Weiner, G. (1992) Staffing Policies in Further and Higher Education: Setting the Scene. Paper given at the Equal Opportunities and Management Symposium, CEDAR annual conference, University of Warwick, April.

Firestone, S. (1970) *Dialectic of Sex.* New York, Paladin.

Foucault, M. (1974) *The Archaeology of Knowledge.* London, Tavistock.

Freire, P. (1972) *Pedagogy of the Oppressed.* London, Penguin.

Friedan, B. (1963) *The Feminine Mystique.* Harmondsworth, Penguin.

Fulford, R. (1958) *Votes for Women.* London, Faber & Faber.

Gallop, J., Hirsch, M. and Miller, N.K. (1990) Criticizing feminist criticism. In Hirsch, M. and Fox Keller, E. (eds) *Conflicts in Feminism.* New York, Routledge.

George, R. (1993) *Equal Opportunities in Schools: Principles, Policy and Practice.* Harlow, Longman.

Gilbert, R. (1989) Text analysis and ideology critique of curricular content. In Castell *et al.* (eds) *Language, Authority and Criticism.* London, Falmer Press.

Gill, D. (1990) Response on behalf of Hackney teachers to the National Curriculum History Working Group Final Report. Unpublished submission to DES.

Goodson, I. (1981) Life history and the study of schooling, *Interchange, Ontario,* 11 (4).

Gordon, P. (1978) A unity of purpose: Some reflections on the school curriculum 1945–70. In Marsden, W. (ed.) *Post-War Curriculum Development: An Historical Appraisal.* Leicester, History of Education Society.

Gramsci, A. (1971) *Selections from Prison Notebooks.* Edited/translated by Hoare, Q. and Nowell-Smith, G. London, Lawrence & Wishart.

Greer, G. (1970) *The Female Eunuch.* London, Paladin.

Griffin, C. (1985) *Typical Girls.* London, Routledge & Kegan Paul.

Griffiths, M. (1992) Making the Difference: Feminism, Postmodernism and the Methodology of Educational Research. Paper presented to the ESRC seminar, Methodology and Epistemology in Educational Research, Liverpool University, June.

Guerney, M. (1989) Implementer or innovator? A teacher's challenge to the restrictive paradigm of traditional research. In Lomax, P. (ed.)

The Management of Change: BERA Dialogues 1. Clevedon, Multilingual Matters.

Hakim, C. (1987) *Research Design: Strategies and Choices in the Design of Social Research.* London, Unwin Hyman.

Hall, S. (1988) *The Hard Road to Renewal.* London, Verso.

Hamilton, D. (1989) *Towards a Theory of Schooling.* London, Falmer Press.

Hamilton, D. (1990) *Curriculum History.* Geelong, Deakin University Press.

Hamilton, D., Jenkins, D., King, C., MacDonald, B. and Parlett, M. (eds) (1977) *Beyond the Numbers Game.* London, Macmillan.

Handy, C. and Aitken, R. (1986) *Understanding Schools as Organisations.* Harmondsworth, Penguin.

Harding, J. (1983) *Switched Off: The Science Education of Girls.* York, Longman.

Harding, S. (1986) *The Science Question in Feminism.* Ithaca, NY, Cornell University Press.

Harding, S. (ed.) (1987) *Feminism and Methodology.* Milton Keynes, Open University Press.

Harding, S. (1990) Feminism, science and the anti-Enlightenment critiques. In Nicholson, L.J. (ed.) *Feminism/Postmodernism.* New York, Routledge.

Harland, J. (1987) The TVEI experience: Issues of control, response and the professional role of teachers. In Gleason, D. (ed.) *TVEI and Secondary Education: A Critical Appraisal.* Milton Keynes, Open University Press.

Harraway, D. (1990) A manifesto for cyborgs: Science, technology and socialist feminism in the 1990s. In Nicholson, L.J. (ed.) *Feminism/Postmodernism.* New York, Routledge.

Hartmann, H. (1976) Capitalism, patriarchy and job segregation by sex. In Blaxall, M. and Reagan, B. (eds) *Women in the Workplace: The Implications of Occupational Segregation.* Chicago, University of Chicago Press.

Havelock, R.G. (1971) *Planning for Innovation through Dissemination and Utilization of Knowledge,* Ann Arbor, MI, Centre for Research and Utilization of Knowledge.

Hearn, J. and Morgan, D. (eds) (1990) *Men, Masculinity and Social Theory.* London, Hyman Unwin.

Heilbrun, C. (1989) *Writing a Woman's Life.* London, The Women's Press.

Hekman, S.J. (1990) *Gender and Knowledge: Elements of Postmodern Feminism.* Boston, Northeastern University Press.

Her Majesty's Inspectorate (HMI) (1992) *The Preparation of Girls for Adult and Working Life.* London, HMSO.

Hill Collins, P. (1990) *Black Feminist Thought.* New York, Routledge.

Hirsch, M. and Fox Keller, E. (eds) (1990) *Conflicts in Feminism.* New York, Routledge.

Holly, L. (1989) Introduction: The sexual agenda of schools. In Holly, L. (ed.) *Girls and Sexuality: Teaching and Learning*. Milton Keynes, Open University Press.

Home Office (1975) Sex Discrimination Act. London, HMSO.

Home Office (1976) Race Relations Act. London, HMSO.

hooks, b. (1982) *Ain't I a Woman: Black Women and Feminism*. (1992 edn) London, Pluto Press.

hooks, b. (1984) *Feminist Theory: From Margin to Center*. Boston, South End Press.

Hudson, W. (1989) Postmodernity and contemporary social thought. In Lassman, P. (ed.) *Politics and Social Theory*. London, Routledge.

Humm, M. (1989) *The Dictionary of Feminist Theory*. Hemel Hempstead, Harvester, Wheatsheaf.

Inner London Education Authority (1986a) *Primary Matters*. London, ILEA.

Inner London Education Authority (1986b) *Secondary Issues*. London, ILEA.

Jenkins, R. and Solomos, J. (1989) *Racism and Equal Opportunity Policies in the 1980s*. 2nd edn, Cambridge, Cambridge University Press.

Jones, A. (1993) Becoming a 'girl': Post-structuralist suggestions for educational research, *Gender and Education*, 5 (2): 157–66.

Jones, C. and Mahony, P. (1989) *Learning Our Lines: Sexuality and Social Control in Education*. London, The Women's Press.

Kamm, J. (1965) *Hope Deferred*. London, Methuen.

Kelly, A. (ed.) (1981) *The Missing Half: Girls and Science Education*. Manchester, Manchester University Press.

Kelly, A. (1985) Changing schools and changing society: Some reflections on the Girls into Science and Technology project. In Arnot, M. (ed.) *Race and Gender: Equal opportunities policies in education*. Oxford, Pergamon.

Kenway, J. and Modra, H. (1992) Feminist pedagogy and emancipatory possibilities. In Luke, C. and Gore, J. (eds) *Feminisms and Critical Pedagogy*. New York, Routledge.

Kettle, M. (1990) The great battle of history, *The Guardian*, 4 April.

Lather, P. (1991) *Getting Smart: Feminist Research and Pedagogy With/ in the Postmodern*. New York, Routledge.

Lawton, D. (1975) *Class, Culture and the Curriculum*. London, Routledge & Kegan Paul.

Lerner, G. (1981) *The Majority Finds its Past: Placing Women in History*. Oxford, Oxford University Press.

Lewis, M. (1990) Interrupting patriarchy: Politics, resistance and transformation in the feminist classroom, *Harvard Educational Review*, 60 (4): 467–88.

Luke, C. and Gore, J. (1992) Introduction. In Luke, C. and Gore, J. (eds) *Feminisms and Critical Pedagogy*. London, Routledge.

Mac an Ghaill, M. (1991) Schooling, sexuality and male power: Towards an emancipatory curriculum, *Gender and Education*, 3 (3): 291–310.

MacDonald, B. and Walker, R. (1976) *Changing the Curriculum*. London, Open Books.

MacDonald, M. (1981) Schooling and the reproduction of class and gender relations. In Dale, R. *et al.* (eds) *Politics, Patriarchy and Practice*. London, Falmer/Open University.

Maclure, M. (1993) Arguing for your self: Identity as an organising principle in teachers' jobs and lives, *British Educational Research Journal*, 19 (4): 311–22.

MacLure, S. (1990) *Education Re-Formed*. London, Hodder & Stoughton.

McPake, J. (1992) Equal Opportunities Policy Documents in Further and Higher Education: Some Reflections. Paper presented at the annual conference of the British Educational Research Association, Stirling, August.

McRobbie, A. (1978) Working class girls and the culture of femininity. In Women's Studies Group, Centre of Contemporary Cultural Studies (ed.) *Women Take Issue*. London, Hutchinson.

McWilliam, E. (1993) 'Post' haste: Plodding research and galloping theory, *British Journal Of Sociology of Education*, 14 (2): 199–206.

Maitland, S. (1983) *A Map of the New Country: Women and Christianity*. London, Routledge & Kegan Paul.

Marshall, C. (1985) From culturally defined to self defined: Career stages of women administrators, *Journal of Educational Thought*, 19 (2): 134–47.

May, N. and Rudduck, J. (1983) *Sex Stereotyping and the Early Years of Schooling*. Centre for Applied Research in Education, Norwich, University of East Anglia.

Measor, L. and Sikes, P. (1992) *Gender and Schooling*. London, Cassell.

Mernissi, F. (1985) *Beyond the Veil: Male–Female Dynamics in Muslim Society*. London, Al Saqi Books.

Mies, M. (1983) Towards a methodology for feminist research. In Bowles, G. and Duelli Klein, R. (eds) *Theories of Women's Studies*. London, Routledge & Kegan Paul.

Millett, K. (1971) *Sexual Politics*. London, Hart Davis.

Millman, V. (1983) Teacher Research. In Elm Bank Teachers' Centre (ed.) *Equal Opportunities in Secondary Schools: What Does It Mean for Girls?* Coventry, Elm Bank.

Millman, V. (1987) Teacher as researcher: A new tradition for research on gender. In Weiner, G. and Arnot, M. (eds) *Gender Under Scrutiny*. London, Hutchinson.

Millman, V. and Weiner, G. (1985) *Sex Differentiation in Schools: Is There Really a Problem?* York, Longman.

Millman, V. and Weiner, G. (1987) Engendering equal opportunities: The case of TVEI. In Gleason, D. (ed.) *TVEI and Secondary Education: A Critical Appraisal.* Milton Keynes, Open University Press.

Minhas, R. (1986) Race, gender and class – Making the connections. In ILEA (ed.) *Secondary Matters.* London, ILEA.

Ministry of Education (1959) *15–18: A Report of the Central Advisory Council for Education in England* [the Crowther Report]. London, HMSO.

Mirza, H. (1992) *Young, Female and Black.* London, Routledge.

Mitchell, J. (1971) *Woman's Estate.* Harmondsworth, Penguin.

Mitchell, J. (1982) *Psychoanalysis and Feminism.* Harmondsworth, Penguin.

Mitchell, J. (1986) Reflections on twenty years of feminism. In Mitchell, J. and Oakley, A. (eds) *What is Feminism?* Oxford, Blackwell.

Mohamed, S. (1986) Racism and sexism: Positive action across the curriculum. In ILEA, *Primary Matters.* London, ILEA.

Myers, K. (1986) *Genderwatch.* London, SCDC; revised and reprinted in 1992, Cambridge, Cambridge University Press.

National Association of Schoolmasters and Union of Women Teachers (NASUWT) (undated) *ERA and Equal Opportunities for the Teacher: A Practical Guide.* London, NASUWT.

National Curriculum Council (NCC) (1992) *Starting Out with the National Curriculum.* York, NCC.

National Curriculum History Working Group (1990) *Final Report.* London, DES.

National Curriculum Mathematics Working Group (1988) *Final Report.* London, DES.

National Union of Teachers (NUT) (1981) *Promotion and the Woman Teacher.* Manchester, EOC/NUT.

National Union of Teachers (NUT) (1986) *Briefing*, 2, autumn, NUT.

National Union of Teachers (NUT) (1990) *Fair and Equal: Guidelines on Equal Opportunities in the Appointment and Promotion of Teachers.* London, NUT.

Neale, M. (1991) Implementing equal opportunity in a boys' secondary school. In Lomax, P. (ed.) *Managing Better Schools and Colleges: BERA Dialogues 5.* Clevedon, Multilingual Matters.

Nicholson, L.J. (1990) *Feminism/Postmodernism.* New York, Routledge.

Oakley, A. (1981) Interviewing women: A contradiction in terms. In Roberts, H. (ed.) *Doing Feminist Research.* London, Routledge & Kegan Paul.

Office for Standards in Education (Ofsted) (1993) *Curriculum Organisation and Classroom Practice in Primary Schools: A Follow-up Report.* London, DFE.

Open University/Inner London Education Authority (ILEA) (1986) *Girls into Mathematics.* Cambridge, Cambridge University Press.

Oram, A. (1987) Sex antagonism in the teaching profession: Equal pay and the marriage bar 1910–39. In Arnot, M. and Weiner, G. (eds) *Gender and the Politics of Schooling*. London, Hutchinson.

Ord, F. and Quigley, J. (1985) Anti-sexism as good educational practice: What can feminists realistically achieve? In Weiner, G. (ed.) *Just a Bunch of Girls: Feminist Approaches to Schooling*. Milton Keynes, Open University Press.

Ortner, S. (1974) Is female to male as nature to culture? In Rosaldo, M.Z. and Lamphere, L. (eds) *Women, Culture and Society*. Stanford, Stanford University Press.

Phoenix, A. (1987) Theories of gender and black families. In Weiner, G. and Arnot, M. (eds) *Gender Under Scrutiny*. London, Hutchinson.

Popkewitz, T. (1988a) What's in a research project: Some thoughts on the intersection of history, social structure and biography, *Curriculum Enquiry*, 18 (4): 379–400.

Popkewitz, T. (ed.) (1988b) *The Formation of School Subjects*. London, Falmer Press.

Powney, J. (1992) Every Which Way: Comments on Researching Institutional Policy. Paper presented at the annual conference of the British Educational Research Association, Stirling, August.

Powney, J. and Weiner, G. (1991) *Outside of the Norm: Equity and Management in Educational Institutions*. London, South Bank University.

Pring, R. (1989) *The New Curriculum*. London, Cassell.

Probyn, E. (1990) Travels in the postmodern: Making sense of the local. In Nicholson, L.J. (ed.) *Feminism/Postmodernism*. New York, Routledge.

Raggatt, P. (1983) Unit 27: Agencies of Change. In *E204: Purposes and Planning in the Curriculum*. Milton Keynes, Open University Press.

Richards, C. (1978) *Power and the Curriculum: Issues in Curriculum Studies*. Driffield, Nafferton.

Riddell, S. (1989) Exploiting the exploited: The ethics of feminist educational research. In Burgess, R.G. (ed.) *The Ethics of Educational Research*. London, Falmer Press.

Riley, D. (1988) *Am I That Name? Feminism and the Category of 'Women' in History*. Basingstoke, Macmillan.

Rossi, A. (1974) (ed.) *The Feminist Papers: From Adams to de Beauvoir*. New York, Bantam.

Rowbotham, S. (1989) *The Past is Before Us: Feminism in Action since the 1960s*. London, Pandora.

Rumens, C. (1985) (ed.) *Making for the Open: The Chatto Book of Post Feminist Poetry 1964–1984*. London, Chatto & Windus.

Said, E. (1991) *Orientalism: Western Conceptions of the Orient*, originally published 1978. Harmondsworth, Penguin.

Sanders, V. (1989) *The Private Lives of Victorian Women: Autobiography in Nineteenth-century England.* Hemel Hempstead, Harvester Wheatsheaf.

Schon, D. (1971) *Beyond the Stable State: Public and Private Learning in a Changing Society.* Harmondsworth, Penguin.

Schon, D. (1987) *Educating the Reflective Practitioner.* San Francisco, Jossey-Bass.

Schools Council (1979) *Schools Council Internal Report: Annexes A & C 79/297.* unpublished.

Schools Council (1980) *Internal Report: Programme 3 Monitoring and Review Group.* 29 April.

Segal, L. (1987) *Is the Future Female? Troubled Thoughts on Contemporary Feminism.* London, Virago.

Shah, S. (1990) Equal opportunity issues in the context of the national curriculum: A black perspective, *Gender and Education,* 2 (3): 309–318.

Shrewsbury, C.M. (1987) What is Feminist Pedagogy? *Women's Studies Quarterly,* 15 (Fall/Winter).

Shulman, S. (1980) Sex and power: Sexual bases of radical feminism, *SIGNS,* 5 (4): 590–604.

Skilbeck, M. (1989) A changing social and educational context. In Moon, B., Murphy, P. and Raynor J. (eds) *Policies for the Curriculum.* London, Hodder & Stoughton.

Smith, D. (1978) A peculiar eclipsing: Women's exclusion from man's culture, *Women's Studies International Quarterly,* 1: 281–95.

Smith, V. (1990) Split affinities: The use of interracial rape. In Kirsch, M. and Fox Keller E. (eds) *Conflicts in Feminism.* New York, Routledge.

Spender, D. (1980) *Man Made Language.* London, Routledge & Kegan Paul.

Spender, D. (1981) *Men's Studies Modified.* Oxford, Pergamon Press.

Spender, D. (ed.) (1983a) *Feminist Theorists.* London, Women's Press.

Spender, D. (1983b) *There's Always Been a Women's Movement.* London, Pandora Press.

Spender, D. (1987) Education: The patriarchal paradigm and the response to feminism. In Arnot, M. and Weiner, G. (eds) *Gender and the Politics of Schooling.* London, Hutchinson.

Stanley, L. (ed.) (1990) *Feminist Praxis: Research, Theory and Epistemology in Feminist Sociology.* London, Routledge.

Stanley, L. and Wise, S. (1983) *Breaking Out: Feminist Consciousness and Feminist Research.* London, Routledge & Kegan Paul.

Stanley, L. and Wise, S. (1990) Method, methodology and epistemology in feminist research processes. In Stanley, L. (ed.) *Feminist Praxis: Research, Theory and Epistemology in Feminist Sociology.* London, Routledge.

Stanworth, M. (1981) *Gender and Schooling: A study of Sexual Division in the Classroom.* London, Hutchinson.

154   Feminisms in education

Steadman, S., Pearson, C. and Salter, B. (1982) *The Impact and Take Up Project*. London, Schools Council.

Stenhouse, L. (1975) *Introduction to Curriculum Research and Development*. London, Heinemann Education.

Stones, R. (1983) '*Pour out the cocoa, Janet': Sexism in Children's Books*. York, Longman.

Taylor, H. (1985) A local authority initiative on equal opportunities. In Arnot, M. (ed.) *Race and Gender: Equal Opportunities in Education*. Oxford, Pergamon.

Taylor, S. (1991) Equal Opportunities Policies and the 1988 Education Reform Act in Britain: Equity Issues in Cultural and Political Context. Unpublished paper, Queensland University of Technology, Australia.

Taylor, S. (1993) Transforming the texts: Towards a feminist classroom practice. In Christian Smith, L. (ed.) *Texts of Desire: Girls, Popular Fiction and Education*. London, Falmer Press.

Thomas, K. (1990) *Gender and Subject in Higher Education*. Milton Keynes, Open University Press.

Tong, R. (1989) *Feminist Thought: A Comprehensive Introduction*. Sydney, Unwin & Hyman.

Troyna, B. and Carrington, B. (1990) *Education, Racism and Reform*. London, Routledge.

Troyna, B. and Williams, J. (1986) *Racism, Education and the State*. London, Croom Helm.

Tuttle, L. (1986) *Encyclopedia of Feminism*. London, Arrow Books.

Tyler, R. (1949) *Basic Principles of Curriculum and Instruction*. Chicago, University of Chicago Press.

Vidal, J. (1993) And the eco-feminists shall inherit the earth, *The Guardian* (supplement) 9 August: 10.

Walden, R. and Walkerdine, V. (1982) *Girls and Mathematics: The Early Years*. Bedford Way Papers, London University Institute of Education.

Walkerdine, V. (1988) *The Mastery of Reason*. London, Routledge.

Walkerdine, V. (1989) *Counting Girls Out*. London, Virago.

Walkerdine, V. (1990) *School Girl Fictions*. London, Verso.

Wallach Scott, J. (1983) Women in history 2: The modern period, *Past and Present*, 101: 141–57.

Wallach Scott, J. (1988) *Gender and the Politics of History*. New York, Columbia University Press.

Wallach Scott, J. (1990) Deconstructing equality-versus-difference; or the uses of poststructural theory for feminism. In Hirsch, M. and Fox Keller, E. (eds) *Conflicts in Feminism*. Routledge, New York.

WedG (1983) *Women's Education Group Newsletter*, October, London.

Weedon, C. (1987) *Feminist Practice and Poststructuralist Theory*. Oxford, Basil Blackwell.

Weiler, K. (1991) Freire and feminist pedagogy of difference, *Harvard Educational Review*, 61 (4) pp. 449–74.

Weiner, G. (1971) Vida Goldstein and Her Work for the International Suffrage Movement. Unpublished undergraduate project, Sidney Webb College.

Weiner, G. (1976) Girls' Education, the Curriculum and the Sex Discrimination Act. Unpublished MA dissertation, London University Institute of Education.

Weiner, G. (1980) Sex differences in mathematical performance: A review of research and possible action. In Deem, R. (ed.) *Schooling for Women's Work*. London, Routledge & Kegan Paul.

Weiner, G. (1985a) The Schools Council and gender: A case-study of policy making and curriculum innovation. In Arnot, M. (ed.) *Race and Gender: Equal Opportunities Policies in Education*. Oxford, Pergamon.

Weiner, G. (1985b) Equal opportunities, feminism and girls' education: An introduction. In Weiner, G. (ed.) *Just a Bunch of Girls: Feminist Approaches to Schooling*. Milton Keynes, Open University Press.

Weiner, G. (1986) Equal opportunities and feminist education: Unity or discord! *British Journal of Sociology of Education*, 7 (3): 265–74.

Weiner, G. (1989a) Professional self-knowledge versus social justice: A critical analysis of the teacher-researcher movement, *British Educational Research Journal*, 15 (1): 41–51.

Weiner, G. (1989b) Feminism, equal opportunities and vocationalism: The changing context. In Burchell, H. and Millman, V. (eds) *Changing Perspectives on Gender: New Initiatives in Secondary Education*. Milton Keynes, Open University Press.

Weiner, G. (1990) Ethical practice in an unjust world: Educational evaluation and social justice, *Gender and Education*, 2 (2): 231–8.

Weiner, G. (1991a) Controversies and Contradictions: Approaches to the Study of Harriet Martinean (1802–76), unpublished doctoral thesis, Open University.

Weiner, G. (1991b) Shell-Shock or sisterhood! Ideology in the British National Curriculum: School history and feminist practice, *Journal of Thought*, 26 (1–2): 69–94.

Weiner, G. (1992a) Enterprise culture, Victorian values or equality: Ideology in the National Curriculum. *Internationale Schulbuchforschung/ International Textbook Research*, 14: 59–70.

Weiner, G. (1992b) What do I do with the data? Some Thoughts on Institutional Policy Research and Feminist Methodology. Paper presented at the British Educational Research Association, annual conference, Stirling, Scotland, August.

Weiner, G. (1993) Shell-shock or sisterhood: English school history and feminist practice. In Arnot, M. and Weiler, K. (eds) *Feminism and Social Justice in Education*. London, Falmer Press.

Weiner, G. and Arnot, M. (eds) (1987a) *Gender Under Scrutiny*. London, Hutchinson.

Weiner, G. and Arnot, M. (1987b) Teachers and gender politics. In Arnot, M. and Weiner, G. (eds) *Gender and the Politics of Schooling*. London, Hutchinson.

Whyte, J. (1983) *Beyond the Wendy House: Sex Role Stereotyping in Primary Schools*. York, Longman.

Williams, J. (1987) The construction of women and black students as educational problems: Re-evaluating policy on gender and 'race'. In Arnot, M. and Weiner, G. (Eds) *Gender and the Politics of Schooling*. London, Hutchinson.

Willis, P. (1977) *Learning to Labour*. Farnborough, Saxon House.

Wiseman, S. (1967) *Intelligence and Ability*. Harmondsworth, Penguin.

Wollstonecraft, M. (1985) *Vindication of the Rights of Women*, originally published 1792, London, Penguin.

Wolpe, A.M. (1976) The official ideology of education for girls. In Flude, M. and Ahier, J. (eds) *Educability, Schools and Ideology*. London, Croom Helm.

Wolpe, A.M. (1988) *Within School Walls: The Role of Discipline, Sexuality and the Curriculum*. London, Routledge.

Women in the NUT (1981) *Newsletter*, London, NUT.

Women in Higher Education Network (WHEN) (1991) *Access and After: Conference Report*. Nottingham, WHEN.

Women in Education (1982) *Newsletter*, 24, Manchester.

Woods, P. (1993) Managing marginality: Teacher development through grounded life history, *British Educational Research Journal*, 19 (5): 447–65.

Wright, C. (1987) The relations between teachers and Afro-Caribbean pupils: Observing multiracial classrooms. In Weiner, G. and Arnot, M. (eds) *Gender Under Scrutiny*. London, Hutchinson.

Yates, L. (1985) Is girl-friendly schooling really what girls need? In Whyte, J., Deem, R., Kant, L. and Cruickshank, M. (eds) *Girl Friendly Schooling*. London, Methuen.

Young, I.M. (1985) Humanism, Gynocentrism and Feminist Politics, *Women's International Studies Forum*, 8 (3).

Young, M. (1971) *Knowledge and Control: New Directions for the Sociology of Education*. London, Collier-Macmillan.

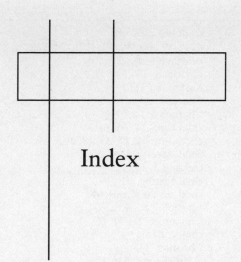

Index